PRAISE FOR LISBETH ZORNIG ANDERSEN'S *ANGER IS MY MIDDLE NAME*

"Heart-wrenching . . . an important testimonial from a Denmark few ever see from within . . . a reminder that if we give a little extra—if we give of ourselves—we might also give a child a chance to rise and break the social curse."

—*Kristeligt Dagblad*

"Although a grim tale, the book is ultimately life-affirming, as it illustrates that it is possible to reject one's negative background and have a good life."

—*Litteratursiden*

"A deeply moving odyssey through the twilight of Denmark's underclass."
—*Politiken*

"Moving in its honesty."

—*Jyllands-Posten*

ANGER
IS MY MIDDLE NAME

ANGER
IS MY MIDDLE NAME

A Memoir

LISBETH ZORNIG ANDERSEN
Translated by Mark Mussari

amazon crossing

ARTICLE 19

1. States Parties shall take all appropriate legislative, administrative, social and educational measures to protect the child from all forms of physical or mental violence, injury or abuse, neglect or negligent treatment, maltreatment or exploitation, including sexual abuse, while in the care of parent(s), legal guardian(s) or any other person who has the care of the child.

United Nations Convention on the Rights of the Child

Contents

PROLOGUE

Sometimes I think about my life when I was a filthy, unwanted kid from Copenhagen living out in the country and roaming around Lolland with my three older brothers. One summer we took off on our bikes and rode all the way to the local beach at Hestehovedets Harbor, near Nakskov. I must have been eight at the time. I sat on the back of my brothers' bikes. We swam in our underwear, dried ourselves off with our sweaters, and then rode home again. No one even knew we had gone. We didn't bring any food with us—we didn't even have any blankets like the other people swimming. But we knew where you could pick apples and berries along the way. A lovely summer memory of a time when my brothers were protecting me, but also a memory of a childhood without the boundaries every child needs. A childhood characterized for many years by betrayal, violence, and sexual assault, all of which formed the person I am today. A person who defies authority without blinking yet is still afraid to sleep with the lights off—who gets dry mouthed when she has to renew her passport. Who'd have thought that I would ever enter the world of politics and become a spokesperson for children?

One evening in 2009, after many years of working full-time as an IT programmer and business developer, I came home tired and exhausted, as usual. With groceries in both hands and my computer bag slung over my shoulder, I fought my way through the hallway, which was overflowing with my children's and their friends' shoes. For once I didn't yell that the children needed to get their shoes out of there if they wanted to keep them. Instead, I just sat down at the kitchen table and stared at the scene. I counted six children. My daughter Ida stood out—there was something different about her. Did she have that many ear piercings when I left for work that morning—and that hair color? I suddenly realized that I'd been working too much and knew too little about my own children's lives.

The next day I quit my job. Although it was the most exciting I'd ever had, it demanded my constant attention, and I gave it my all, from early morning to late at night. So, while it was a huge relief to quit, it was also incredibly stressful to go freelance and worry about not finding enough work. About getting sick. About not being good enough. The constant angst that had followed me since my early childhood.

I started working as a self-employed IT and management consultant and subcontractor for the Danish company Zangenberg. At home, I became much more present as a mother. I was also earning more money, so I could give my family bigger gifts and we could travel more. I spent most of my time at Zangenberg sitting alone, deep in research and analysis, at an elegant desk in an all-white office in a tony neighborhood.

Early one morning I checked my phone to find a voice message from Henrik Lund, the personal secretary to Karen Ellemann, then Denmark's recently appointed Minister of Social Affairs and Secretary of the Interior. Lund asked me to call him back, which I did while wondering why a minister's secretary was calling me. He told me the minister was inviting me for coffee because she wanted to hear a little about my life and discuss a few things. I inquired a bit more about it, and Lund said it concerned my experience being institutionalized during my childhood.

We scheduled a meeting at the ministry for a week later: Friday afternoon, November 6, 2009.

When the day for having coffee with the minister finally arrived, Henrik showed me into the minister's office. Smiling broadly, Karen Ellemann stood there, her hand extended. We sat down, Karen poured some coffee, and I waited anxiously. Karen said that she had read a feature written by Karen Gjesing and me in the magazine *Danish Communities*. The article, by then a few years old, was the result of an evening Karen and I had spent talking about finding some use for our shared history.

Karen Gjesing had been my social worker at Hylleholt Residence for Girls: I was a wild fourteen-year-old who'd escaped western Lolland and had wound up at a treatment center for young girls with behavioral problems. In the article, Karen wrote about investing oneself in other people's children; I used my background as an economist with a degree from the University of Copenhagen to create a business case study that laid out what my brother Tonny and I had both cost and contributed to society. The report compared Tonny's time in institutions, which hadn't done him much good, and his long criminal record of drug and alcohol abuse, to the massive investment in me, including time at a special institution with a high percentage of well-educated social workers and other practitioners, many hours of psychological treatment, and rehabilitation benefits through the entire educational system.

Karen Ellemann explained that she was attracted to the idea that civil society, certain individuals, had probably made the biggest difference for me. I agreed—but I added that a lot of money had been invested in me in the form of treatment and education, which were also important. We dove into an intense conversation about personal responsibility and vulnerable children and teenagers. Along the way, she told me about her own life as an elementary school teacher and a divorced career woman with joint custody of her children.

Suddenly she asked what I knew about the National Council for Children. I stared at her. The National Council for Children? I replied that I didn't know much about it and that I was more focused on at-risk teens. She responded that the National Council for Children covers children up to the age of eighteen and monitors whether Denmark is complying with the UN Convention on the Rights of the Child, while also acting as a spokesperson for children.

"Exciting," I said, wondering why she'd brought it up.

She told me they were searching for a chairperson for the National Council and she was offering me the post, saying that I represented our nation's most vulnerable in a way the council had never seen before. I had no idea how to respond and felt as if I needed to say something clever. Instead, I asked if there was any information about the National Council I could look at.

"Yes," she replied. "You can look at their website—and here are some things I've printed out for you."

Karen gave me the weekend to think about the offer, along with her cell-phone number in case there was anything I wanted to discuss. I thanked her, stood up, and left. On my way out of the ministry, I called Karen Gjesing to tell her about the job offer and ask if she thought I should take it.

"Damn! Chair of the National Council for Children!" she exclaimed. "Yes—of course!"

I accepted the offer. For the next three years I served as chair of the National Council for Children, throwing myself into politics and appearing almost daily in both print and broadcast media. I met frequently with members of the Danish parliament, where I fought to strengthen children's rights and to work those rights into legislation—including placing greater focus on the authorities' responsibility for children's well-being, holding meetings with the Catholic church about ethical guidelines for priests, and ensuring Denmark's compliance with the UN Convention on the Rights of the Child at meetings in Geneva. And so much more.

Who would have ever believed it? Not me.

This book is not about my time as chair of the National Council for Children, however: it is about my childhood, which qualified me for the job. I invite you to join me on a journey to Denmark's darker side—to an everyday life filled with abuse and violence at a level only few can imagine. I've chosen to share my story to illustrate how a child experiences a truly terrible upbringing. When I was chair of Denmark's National Council for Children, I met many children living the same unfortunate life my brothers and I experienced. My role was to serve as a spokesperson for those children—for all children, including the most vulnerable. Whether you're a neighbor, a social worker, a schoolteacher, or a grandparent, you must and should act. In this book, you'll meet many people who acted on my behalf. I hope they will inspire you to reach out as well.

At the same time, I hope the book will impart some wisdom to adults, both young and old, who've also been abused. They'll recognize themselves in scenes they've possibly never told anyone about because of their shame, guilt, and sorrow. Hopefully they'll discover that they can still lead normal—even good—lives. I hope my tale will help professionals who work with children—as well as adults who've experienced safe and happy childhoods—understand the damage that can be done to vulnerable children and adults.

I've tried to describe what I remember of my early childhood. Therefore, the story develops in both language and perspective as I get older. The first chapters are almost unreflective descriptions of events in which I don't relate to what happened. I simply recount what I remember, have been told, or have read in my case files. Later chapters contain some of the reflections I recall having at a specific age. I didn't include all incidents or events—only a selection to offer the basic tenor of my everyday childhood.

I chose this style because I wanted to give the child Lisbeth a credible voice, which I could not achieve if I told my story in the rationalizing voice of an adult. Still, I've cheated a bit by using photo captions to supply the adult voice relating past incidents.

Throughout the book, I've tried to stick to descriptions rather than judgments. Some people from my past will feel singled out, but I can't describe the realities of my life if I omit what's offensive. The people who assaulted me know who they are: now they will have to face the fact that the rest of the world also knows that they abused at least one child, just as I must live as an adult who was abused.

A little about memory: I realize that I might recall things imprecisely—everyone does—but I haven't changed the text because of it. What I recall is the reality I experienced, the one that shaped me—that still shapes me—as a person.

Recognizing that I may have forgotten things, or remembered them incorrectly, I've strengthened my memory by seeking access to my personal files and by interviewing most of the people about whom I've written. I have included a few of those documents in this book. Director Mette Korsgaard, from Krage Film, documented some of these interviews on camera in *My Childhood in Hell* (*Min barndom i helvede*). The documentary follows my efforts to understand my childhood: it shows how I was able to break free from my social inheritance.

My mother and father know what I have written—that I have written about both their love and failure. I haven't asked for their permission. They chose to take part in the documentary to explain themselves. I believe they accept the book as an honest account of my brothers' and my childhood, which they have not always been part of.

At the time that I wrote this book, two of my brothers knew about it; I asked for their blessing to write about them, and they granted it. My stepfather acknowledges the abuse, but claims not to recall if it was also of a sexual nature.

"Zornig"—my middle name—means "angry" in German. Except for the gratitude I've felt for the help of so many friendly people, anger has been the driving force in my life. I hope that, with time, I can let go of it altogether. Until then, anger is my middle name—for better or worse.

1968–71

Mom and Dad are beautiful. They're both blond and thin. Mom often wears short skirts or shorts and high boots in a matching color. It's the height of fashion—and Mom likes to look chic. Some people say she resembles the Swedish singer Anniqa. Dad often wears white shirts, which he uses when he works as a waiter. He has thick, wavy hair and eyes that are always smiling. I love my father's eyes.

Now and then we visit Grandma and Grandpa, who live nearby in a red wooden house. Grandpa mostly just lies in bed since he broke his leg, although he gets up sometimes to take his three-wheel moped to the pub. Before Grandpa got hurt, he used to go down to the harbor every morning to try to find work. He usually got paid in cash, but sometimes they paid him in fish. That's why Mom hates fish.

Grandma and Grandpa's house always smells like gas, petroleum, boiled potatoes, and dogs. The house has a living room, a kitchen, two bedrooms, and an attic. And there's a small bathroom with no sink. The bathroom floor bulges and turns up at the edges. And it always smells like pee.

One of the bedrooms is Grandpa's. He has his bed, a standing ashtray, a police radio, a walkie-talkie, and his beloved parrot, Jakob. Jakob has his own bag of peanuts next to his cage. Grandpa lies there every day in a fog, smoking with his cigarette holder. Sometimes he yells at

Grandma in the living room when he wants coffee or a beer, and then Grandma yells back, "Shut up, you old fool," and laughs.

Sometimes I go into Grandpa's room. Not to talk to Grandpa—I'm afraid of him. He coughs all the time, speaks in a rusty voice, and is cross-eyed. But I like to talk to Jakob, who can sing the old Danish song: "That time when I left home, Jakob came along."

Grandma's room has a single bed, a double bed, and a closet. When I stay over, I sleep with Grandma in the double bed. Next to her bed is a nightstand with a small radio that plays music all night long and a soda bottle with a cork in it. Grandma always keeps a red or green soda on the nightstand. Every evening she takes one sip and then puts the cork back in. Jens sleeps in the other bed. He's my cousin, the son of my uncle Pjevs. Jens lives with Grandma and Grandpa.

I've never been in the attic. I wouldn't dare. That's where Putte lives. He's one of my uncles. Sometimes he comes running into the house to hide from the police. Then Grandma says he isn't home.

The kitchen is small and narrow and smells like gas from the stove and the white water heater hanging over the sink. This is where we wash ourselves too. In the doorway to the kitchen there's a curtain you can pull closed when you need to wash up. The pot for potatoes sits on the gas stove. There's a gray ring of dried potato foam on the inside of the pot. When she needs to make dinner, Grandma fills the big pot with potatoes and water and carries it into the living room. Then she sits down by the coffee table with the pot in her lap and peels the potatoes.

Grandma and Grandpa have two dogs, Døtter and Chap. I like to lie down on the floor with Døtter and bury my nose in her stomach while I listen to the adults talking. The wood floor in the living room is shiny and greasy. From the floor, I can look up at the coffee table, which is covered with ashtrays and coffee cups, cream in a brown pitcher, and a sugar bowl with sugar cubes in it. And there's a huge thermos with a spigot on the side and a button on top you can push to get coffee. There are usually a lot of beer bottles on the table too. Grandma never drinks beer, but Grandpa and many of their guests do. Under the table there's an orange rug with long tufts. If you look closely enough, you can see a whole field of brown tobacco in between the tufts. It's tobacco from all the adults who roll cigarettes. Grandma and Grandpa always have a lot of guests.

Mom was eighteen when she married Dad. They're from the same neighborhood in South Harbor. She told me that they became sweethearts one day when Dad and one of his friends were teasing Mom about missing some teeth. She gave him a good smack, as she says, and then they became sweethearts. She was already pregnant by another man with my older brother Michael at that time, but Dad says that they got married because it was one way to leave home and get your own apartment.

Dad is the second of four children. My father's mother was named Vonne, and my father's father was Alfred. I've been told they both died at the age of forty-nine from alcohol abuse.

Mom is the fifth of eight children; she had two other siblings who died at birth. According to Dad, Mom's three younger siblings were all mentally handicapped, and they each lived at Ebberødgård, an institution, at various times as children. So my mother was often the youngest child at home. Mom says she was expelled from school in seventh grade for hitting the other children. My father is to the left in the picture.

All of my brothers are bigger than me. René is three years older, Tonny is four years older, and Michael is five years older. They don't play with me much, but I'm always somewhere near them. My brothers spend most of their time outdoors, and whenever I'm allowed to, I go out with them. The dogs have dug up Grandma and Grandpa's garden, so there are small piles of dirt and holes in the ground. On one side of the garden is a large vacant lot where grass and weeds grow wild. Some old junk cars and a couple of mobile homes with people living in them are scattered around. A hillside where the train tracks run borders the area. When you're sitting inside, you can hear the windows rattle as the train goes by. I like that sound. My brothers like to run close to the train, but I don't dare.

We live on Händelsvej in South Harbor with Mom and Dad. We sleep in two bunk beds in the apartment, which has two bedrooms and a living room. It smells like cigarette smoke, and the apartment is small and dark. Mom and Dad often have guests, and the adults usually get drunk. Then Mom and Dad fight.

One night when there are a lot of people in the house, I can't find Mom. I walk around looking for her. Suddenly I see Dad bent over Mom out in the hallway while he's yelling angrily down at her. He's holding the back of his head as if he's in pain. Mom is lying totally still on the floor. I scream loudly and run over to her, but a woman I don't know pulls me away from Mom while another closes the door to the hallway. I scream, hit, and bite to try to get to my mother, but the woman holds on tight. I can't see my brothers, and I'm afraid my mother is dead.

Shortly after that, my brothers and I are taken to an orphanage called Kastanjegården. I'm three years old. I find out that I've been in an orphanage before. Once when I was a baby, and then again a year ago. I can't really remember it, but my brothers can. They look forward to it. They say you can play by the water, but first you have to crawl down a cliff.

Kastanjegården is far out in the country, next to a large bridge, and it takes several hours to get there. Mom says that she lived there too, with some of her siblings, when she was little and that it's a good place. And then she tells us that we'll come home again soon.

The drive there is exciting. Uncle Benny is driving. The place looks like a nice old farm, and you can see the sea right behind it. Mom follows us in and a woman greets us. The walls are all painted white, and just inside the door there's an office with glass windows looking out to the hallway. Mom says goodbye and leaves, and all four of us wave as they drive away.

René and I will be living with some girls in a dormitory, where René will be the only boy. Tonny and Michael laugh, which makes René angry, but there's nothing he can do about it. There aren't enough places in the boys' dormitory, and he's the youngest of the three boys. I'm glad he'll be sleeping with me. The girls' dormitory is bright and nice and it smells like oatmeal with sugar on it. They show us our beds, which have white sheets on them. The woman brings us some clothes. The boys have to wear blue overalls, and the girls red.

After a few hours of being allowed to walk around on our own, it's dinnertime. All the children gather in one big dining hall, where we eat at long tables. Best of all, there's a TV hanging beneath the ceiling at one end of the room. So we get to watch children's shows after we eat. I like the food, and I'm full and happy by the time they turn on the TV. While watching *Ingrid and Little Brother*, I fall asleep at the dining table with my head on my arms. A nice adult wakes me up and carries me to my bed.

I lie still beneath the comforter and watch how the other girls and René go to bed. First they have to brush their teeth at a long sink with a lot of faucets. Then they put on their pajamas, and finally they have to pee into a pot in the middle of the dormitory floor. I have to also. I hop out of bed, tiptoe over, pee, and then walk back to bed. Then it's René's turn. He doesn't want to pee in front of girls, but he has to. All the girls are sitting on their beds, cheering him on and laughing, until he finally sits down while he stares at the floor. After a very long time, we can hear him peeing into the pot. René cries while he pees, which makes me cry too. The next night, René pees on the pot without crying. I'm happy to see it.

All the days at Kastanjegården are the same. I keep mostly to myself, close to my brothers. I don't play with the other children, who are all bigger than me, but that doesn't matter. I have my brothers, and I have games inside my head. I love breakfast, but my favorite time of day is dinner, when we watch children's shows together. The only time I'm really sad is the day the orphanage runs out of red overalls that will fit me, so I have to wear blue.

My brothers are not as happy. One day when it's rainy, and we're all outside with our blue and red raincoats on, Michael has to pee. He runs into the bathroom, but he can't figure out how to unbutton his overalls. Finally he pees his pants. As punishment, he has to wear a dress that night, and they put his hair up in a rubber band. Then he has to walk up and down the boys' hallway while all the boys laugh at him. Tonny and René think it's funny, but I don't.

After some time at the orphanage, they tell us that Mom is coming to visit. We can't wait. She shows up one afternoon when it's sunny. We're allowed to sit in one of the offices so we can be alone with her without the other children around. She's carrying a big bag, and we can see packages sticking up out of it. Mom can't wait to give them to us— and neither can we. So, before she gets coffee and we get juice, she starts to hand out packages. I'm excited as I unpack mine. It's a mechanical monkey holding cymbals. When you turn the key in its back, it walks while banging the cymbals together. I've never seen anything like it before, and I can't get enough of making it walk and play, even though the others get angry with me because of all the noise. I don't care. I love my monkey.

After a few hours, Mom has to leave again. This time I cry loudly, as do my brothers. We want to go home with her, but we can't today. Soon, she says. She gives each of us a hug before she gets into the car. Once the car is gone, we go back in to get our toys, but an adult tells us that children aren't allowed to play with their own toys at the orphanage. The children destroy each other's things, so she's packed them into a box that we'll get when we go back home with Mom. I start to cry again. I really wanted to play with the monkey Mom gave me. The adult takes me by the arm and leads me into the playroom.

My mother with Michael, Tonny, René, and me. We are probably around three, six, seven, and eight years old—about the same time Mom and Dad divorced. I remember that this picture was taken right after all four of us took a bath. I eventually inherited the underwear my brothers are wearing.

The big day arrives. We're going home. Since early morning, we've been waiting in our own clothes. I've been standing with my nose pressed against the window for hours. We're finally going home to Mom and

Dad. Our things are packed and ready to go by the door—including the box with our own toys. We can't unpack it till we get home. When Mom and Uncle Benny finally show up, we run into their arms. All the way home we're speaking happily, all at the same time. Dad isn't there when we get home. He's at work. Some of Mom's friends are visiting, and the living room is soon full of cigarette smoke and adults toasting each other.

Because Dad works a lot as a waiter in the afternoons and evenings, we don't see him very often. One evening while he's at work, Mom wakes us up and tells us to get up and put on our clothes. She says we're going for a drive and that a taxi is waiting outside, so we have to hurry. When we get to the car, we see a man standing there waiting. He has a lot of reddish-brown hair, long red sideburns, and eyes that sit deep in his head beneath big, bushy eyebrows. Eyes that burn. Mom says: "This is Jan—he's going to be your father now. We're driving to Køge, where he has a nice big house we're all going to live in."

1971–72

The sun is shining when I wake up the next morning. It's summer and it's hot. The row house we've slept in smells like wood and new paint. My brothers and I sleep in two bunk beds in the same room, and as usual René and I take the lower bed in each one. While I slept I forgot why I'm here, but as I slowly wake up, I remember the drive in the car with the strange man and Mom sitting next to him. They talked the whole way here. In a happy voice, Mom told us that she and Jan met through a personals ad and that we were going to start a new life with a new school for the boys and a house with a garden.

My brothers are still sleeping. I tiptoe out of the room and, as quietly as possible, start to explore the house. It has two bedrooms, a kitchen, a bathroom, and a large living room. I walk out into the garden. It's so nice that you can do that. There are small gardens on each side, separated by a high hedge.

I go back into the house and open a door to a room where Mom and my new father, Jan, are in bed. I look at them for a little while and then go to wake up my brothers.

Jan is a bricklayer, but he doesn't work. He's big and round. Not fat, but round. He has round cheeks, strong arms and legs with a lot of hair all over them, wide hands, a big head with sideburns that go all the way down to his chin, and deep-set eyes that stare out below very strong eyebrows. Both his sideburns and his eyebrows are redder than his big, unruly hair. He always looks like he's scowling, and when he's drunk, it's even worse. I'm really afraid of his eyes.

Soon we're dealing with his anger every day. There are rules and they must be obeyed. If not, we get our pants pulled down and are laid across his lap for a spanking. I'm good at understanding the rules. My brothers are less good at it, especially Tonny, who breaks the rules quite often. For example, we're not allowed to talk while we're eating. We have to eat in complete silence. Mom and Jan don't talk to each other either. It's called eating in peace. The only sound we hear is from the TV at the end of the table. Jan sits at one end of the coffee table as we eat. He's the one who decides what we eat—and how much of it. And we have to eat everything. It's forbidden to leave anything on our plates. If we do, we're punished and thrown into bed. Then we get served what we didn't eat at the next meal.

I cry when my brothers get hit. As we get to know Jan better, my brothers start to bargain with each other over who will take the blame for what Jan discovers. Often Tonny takes the blame—and the beatings. They usually agree to that, but more and more often René decides to blame Tonny, even when they haven't agreed to it. Because René is good at explaining and Tonny isn't, Jan usually believes René's explanations. Michael is the one who eventually talks to René and Tonny about what's reasonable, and he often gets René and Tonny to be friends again. Michael is a true big brother. He makes all the decisions, because he's the oldest, strongest, and wisest. Mom never hits us. But she doesn't defend us either.

One day everything goes wrong. Tonny finds five kroner on the table in the living room and walks over to the grocery store to buy a big bag of caramels. René and Michael see him walking with the bag back to the house, and René runs home yelling that Tonny stole some

money and bought candy with it. Jan and Mom get angry. Jan says that
Tonny took his last five kroner, which he was going to use to take the
bus to the employment center and sign up for unemployment. Tonny
comes merrily walking down the garden path with the bag in his hand.
Jan runs right up to him. He drags him by the hair into the house, and
then I hear violent smacks as Jan's hands hit Tonny's rear end. It lasts
for a long time—longer than normal. Tonny cries and keeps yelling that
he's sorry. After a while, Tonny comes back out, red eyed and sniffling,
with the bag of caramels in his hand. He doesn't look at us—he just
walks back down the garden path. He's going back to the grocer's to
return the caramels so Jan can get his five kroner back.

Tonny is seven years old. He doesn't look like the rest of us and he seems
different. He behaves strangely, never thinks twice, and has a hard time
learning anything. He has Dad's smiling eyes, but otherwise he looks
different. He has an egg-shaped head, and he's usually smiling.

Tonny returns happily with the five kroner. I'm surprised he was
able to get all the money back, since he ate some of the caramels. Then
Jan heads to Køge to sign up for his unemployment check.

We're always out of money, so Jan and Mom try to save on everything. For example, they bought three gigantic wine carboys that they
keep in the living room. Now and then the bottles give off a sound. A
plop. They're brewing wine in them, so they have something to drink.
And they roll their own cigarettes because that's cheaper too.

Mom makes cigarettes with filters, just like Grandma and Grandpa.
But Jan uses a tiny machine with two rollers and a red mat that's pulled
down over the rollers. I think it's fun to watch him do it, and once I
was allowed to try. He sat behind me with his hands and arms around
me to guide my movements. He smelled like wine and cigarettes, and
his breath was hot and sour. His rough sideburns scratched against
my cheek. I tried to do it quickly, so I could get away from him. The

cigarette fell apart when I opened the mat and the rollers. Jan laughed and said we'll have to practice some more. Now he always wants me to lick the paper while he holds the mat.

I have no playmates, so I play by myself while my brothers are at school. One day they sprint into the garden yelling that some big boys from school are chasing them. I'm sitting outside digging in the ground with a spoon. It's summer—I'm five years old and naked, except for the clogs I'm wearing. Mom and Jan are sitting outside on the patio. Soon a small group of boys is standing on the sidewalk, calling my brothers chickens and telling them to come out and get a beating. I don't know why Michael doesn't come out and make them go away. I get angry and want them to get lost. So I run along the garden path to the boys, and once I've reached them, I take off one of my clogs and hit the closest boy in the face with the heel. I get him right on the nose, which starts to bleed. That makes the boys beat it. As I walk back down the garden path, my brothers, Mom, and Jan are cheering.

Mom and Jan get drunk almost every day. We rarely have guests, and Mom and Jan fight a lot. Sometimes our other grandma—Jan's mother—comes over. She always cleans up when she's here, and she makes wonderful food.

At some point Dad comes to see us with his new wife, Anita. She's eighteen years old and very beautiful. She has dark wavy hair, freckles, soft lips, and the whitest teeth you've ever seen. She has large, smiling brown eyes and she smells nice. Anita doesn't drink or smoke—and she's wearing really nice clothes. I'm crazy about Anita, and I can tell she likes me too.

Anita is from South Harbor and she has four sisters. She's the youngest. Her mother's name is Nancy. They call her "Nangsy." They have a mobile home they keep out in the country, and Dad and Anita take us there. It's the first time I've ever seen the inside of a mobile home. It's gigantic and totally new. Nancy says they have to attach it to a truck to move it every winter. A regular car can't drive with it. Dad takes all of us on a fishing trip at the lake near the campgrounds. He shows us how to put worms on a hook and what to do if you catch a fish.

It's wonderful to be with Dad and Anita. I wish we could live with them. The only problem is that I don't know what to call Dad. When I want his attention, I try to avoid calling him "Dad," because Jan is my father now. My brothers don't have this problem. They just call him "Dad," but I can't get myself to do it. What if Jan finds out? One time when I have to call for my real dad, I call him "Father." He looks at me and says: "Why are you calling me that?" I tell him I don't know.

Tonny and René pretend they're in a rock band. I'm standing on the arm of our sofa, and Jan is holding me while we dance to the music. My clothes are filthy; the pants are too big and the shirt is too small. This scene perfectly illustrates the unpredictability that was our everyday life. Sometimes my brothers got beaten for making too much noise, but if Jan had been drinking and was in a good mood, he would dance with us. Notice the weapons on the wall behind us.

In the fall Mom and Jan tell us that the whole family is going to move so Jan can get a job. We find out that Mom has to have her knee operated on first, because she has damaged cartilage in it. Once that's happened, we'll all move to Lolland. Mom says that we'll drive over the bridge we could see from Kastanjegården. They've bought a white farmhouse with a thatched roof and there's a big garden where you can grow vegetables. As we start to pack, I come across our red photo album and leaf through it. Suddenly I see a picture of Mom and Jan. Jan has on a shirt with a big collar. He's smiling widely with his round cheeks. My mother is standing next to Jan in her white bride's dress. She's holding a beautiful bouquet and has a small crown of flowers with a short veil on her head. She's also smiling. I can see her gold tooth, which she inherited from her grandfather and had melted down so it would fit her. Mom and Jan are married. I didn't know that—but it explains why my brothers say that our name is Nygård now and not Andersen.

I think I know which day they got married. It was the first time I was going to be alone at Grandma and Grandpa's for a few days. Mom took me there. The next day Anita came. Suddenly she was standing in the doorway with Grandma. She and Grandma said it was a surprise for Dad and that I mustn't tell Mom I would be sleeping at Dad and Anita's. I really wanted to go with Anita.

Anita made cold buttermilk soup, and she and I had fun until it was time for me to go to bed. Dad was at work, so I was asleep when he came home. Anita tucked me in on the sofa in the living room, and I was fast asleep until I heard Dad's key in the door. I had butterflies at the thought of Dad finding me on the sofa. I could hear Anita in the hallway telling him he should be very quiet, sneak into the living room, and guess who was lying there. I pretended I was asleep. I could hear them come back into the living room, and I felt Dad leaning over me.

Anita whispered: "See who it is?"

"Yes, it's Eva," Dad replied. Eva is Dad's little sister.

"No," said Anita. "It's Lisbeth. Can't you tell?"

"No," said Dad.

They tiptoed into the kitchen, but I couldn't fall asleep again. I was sad that Dad didn't know who I was.

Finally, one fall day, we move to Lolland, to a town called Nordlunde, just outside of Nakskov. Because Mom just had her knee operated on, she's walking with crutches. On the day we're moving, an ambulance arrives with a stretcher Mom can lie on. The four of us are allowed to sit in back with her. Two ambulance people are sitting up front. None of us has ever been inside an ambulance before, so we're ecstatic about riding in one. And when the ambulance people turn on the siren just for us, we all cheer loudly. I can't imagine a better way to move. Jan drove ahead in the moving truck, so he could be there to meet us when we arrive.

1972–74

Our new home is a small, whitewashed, half-timbered house. The whitewash is flaking off in some places, and the straw roof is all gray, sticks out everywhere, and has holes in it. The gigantic garden has pear, apple, and plum trees, and there are bushes with red currants, gooseberries, and black currants on them. There's a chicken yard too, with some white chickens and a big red rooster.

The potty pail has to be emptied at the far end of the garden. My brothers have to dig holes and empty the bucket, but sometimes they step in the newly dug holes. When that happens, they have to wear dirty shoes and pants for hours before they're allowed to change. Eventually they make a game out of it: they hang a big rope from a tree and then take turns to see who can swing from one end to the other without falling into one of the holes.

A stream twists and turns around the house. It's several yards down to the water, and I'm terrified of falling down there. But this soon becomes my brothers' favorite place to play—it's also where they smoke the cigarettes they steal from Mom and Jan, or from the guests who visit.

Inside, the house has one big bedroom and a smaller one, a tiny living room, a hallway, and a kitchen. There's no toilet or bathroom. The toilet is outside. There's just a wide, worn-out board that runs from one wall of the outhouse to the other, with a hole in the middle. In front, where you hang your legs, is a door you can open to get to the potty pail. On the board there's a roll of hard brown toilet paper that has to be crumpled up and rubbed together a lot so it doesn't scratch. There are some old newspapers there too, which you can use if you run out of toilet paper.

You can both bake in and cook on the wood-burning stove in the kitchen. Over by the stove is a row of hooks for hanging large pots and other things. You can only get cold water from the faucet, so if you want hot water, it has to come from the large black pot that's always on the stove. To take a bath, you have to place a big plastic tub in the middle of the floor. Then a lot of water is boiled for the tub. We take turns bathing in the same water, so it's all about being allowed to go first. We usually take turns.

There's a green stove in one corner of the little living room to keep us warm. Other than that, there's only enough room for our dark-brown leather sofa, four stools, and a small easy chair, all placed around a dark-brown coffee table with dark-blue glazed tiles. The chair sits at the end of the table closest to the stove. At the other end of the coffee table is our black-and-white TV, which is always on. We usually watch the German channels and a lot of music programs, such as *Disco* and *Hitparade*. We all cheer loudly when Gitte Hænning and Dorthe Kollo are on TV. We also watch skiing and a lot of Danish films. Poul Reichhardt and *The Olsen Gang* are the best—and *The House in Christianshavn*.

The smallest room is Mom and Jan's bedroom. It has a double bed and a bookcase with a drawer at the bottom. One day my brothers show me that the drawer is full of magazines with pictures of adults having sex. That's nothing new to me. I hear Mom and Jan having sex and making hard smacking noises—Mom squeals loudly while Jan makes deep sounds. I know what they're doing. I've seen it when I've gone into their bedroom and they don't know I'm there. I've seen Mom on all fours on top of the bed while Jan shoves hard against her backside, again and again. Their backs were to me, and I could see Jan's rear end wrinkle up and get dimples every time he bumped against Mom.

In the magazines, I can see how other people do it. Some pages in *The Weekly Rapport* don't have anything to do with sex. Instead, there are pictures of dead people who've been hanged, houses that are burning, and other things I don't like looking at. I often have nightmares about those pictures.

Our two bunk beds and a closet with our clothes are in the largest room. Our toys are in there too. My brothers have a box with Matchbox cars that I love to play with. The only one I never touch is the English double-decker bus. It used to be red, but Tonny sucked the paint off and now it's gray. He can sit for hours with that toy in his mouth. Now it smells like bad breath and metal. I don't know how he can stand to sit there with it in his mouth—it smells so awful. We laugh at him whenever he does it. I have some girls' toys too. A dollhouse with furniture, a doll, and a doll's bed with a canopy.

Jan says he's going to build some rooms for us so we can each have our own bedroom. First he has to take care of the garden, though, so he can grow enough vegetables to save money on food. My brothers have to dig up the garden. I love to be with them out there. The ground is black and it's like clay, so with a little water you can get it to stick. I make cakes and other kinds of play food that I let dry in the sun. Then I decorate them with dandelions and stones from the garden path.

We buy chicks, goslings, and young doves for breeding, so we have enough meat. Twice a year we also buy a pig that gets carved up. Parts of the pig are cut into smaller pieces and frozen. Other parts get chopped up in a silver-colored grinder with a crank handle that can also be used to make sausage. I love to watch as Jan holds the end of the intestine in one hand while he turns the crank with the other. The intestine slowly fills up with ground meat—and suddenly you have sausage. The trick is to make sure the intestine doesn't tear along the way, or else you have to start all over again.

If the intestine tears, it gets tossed on the floor, where our three dogs—Sussi, Bulder, and Tina—are waiting. Our cats, Pelle and Mikkeline, circle around Jan's and Mom's legs. The dogs never take anything off the floor until they're told it's okay. They're afraid of Jan—one look from him and they lie down.

Each day that passes I get angrier that I don't get to go to school. I miss my brothers, and while they're at school, I just sit around waiting for them to come home. I'm always pestering everyone, but Mom says school doesn't accept five-year-olds. There are two schools: a public school called Ravnsborg, where my brothers go, and a private school called Realskolen. After a while, I'm allowed to go to Realskolen. I don't understand why I can't go to Ravnsborg, but Mom says that school thinks I'm too young. But Realskolen wants to take me, and because Jan has promised the school inspector to build a living room for him, I can go to school for free.

We take the school bus every day. It stops at the grocery store, which is ten minutes from our house. The bus stops for kids at different places, including the local inn to pick up the innkeeper's two daughters. They're always dressed nicely. They have long, curly hair tied up in ribbons, and their cheeks are shiny from cream. I want to shine like that too and have loops in my hair, but my hair is short, so that can't happen. After they pick up all the children, the bus drives to the Ravnsborg School and drops some of them off, including my brothers. Then the rest of us are driven to Realskolen.

I don't like my class—and I miss my brothers. The others in class all know each other, so there's no one for me to play with. They call me "Corn Fed" because my round cheeks make my head look fat, even though I'm skinny. And they think I'm gross because I have pink eye and warts on my hands.

I hate my warts. I've counted more than thirty of them between all my fingers, at the base of my nails, and on my palms. Some of them are old and big and have craters in the middle where something that looks like a black wire sometimes sticks up. And I can't get rid of the pink eye. Tonny and I have it all the time, even though we smear ointment on it. When we wake up in the morning, our eyelashes stick together, and if we scratch them, our eyelashes fall off. I think my eyes look like pig eyes when they're all red and have no eyelashes.

One day I find out that I can go to Ravnsborg. Mom went to the local authorities and talked to our caseworker, Bent, who often helps us. He's a nice man, fat with a red face, and good to talk to. I can tell that he really likes Mom.

Before long, I start kindergarten at Ravnsborg. It's a gigantic school with a lot of new buildings. Kindergarten is in the old school building, which has big rooms and high ceilings. My brothers are in one of the other buildings. I don't mind—I know I can find them during recess. And I love my class. Both the teacher and the other students are nice to me.

My brothers are having a hard time at school. They're usually together during recess, when they have to defend themselves against the kids who call us "snobs from Copenhagen," but they're each in their own classes. Michael does all right, whereas René does really well. Still, all three of them have trouble sitting still in class and doing what they're told. And they beat up anyone who teases them. Both René and Tonny have hit their teachers too. One of them was pregnant.

There's always a lot of work to do in the garden. We have to harvest vegetables and pick berries and fruit. In the winter, snow has to be shoveled and wood chopped for the stove. We work during the weekdays, when we aren't in school, and on weekends. We learn how to pick red currants without tearing off each berry individually and how to snip off black currants and gooseberries. I hate plucking gooseberries, because they stick you—and only the very ripe berries taste good. I'd much rather pick red currants, which are sweet, and it's easy to sneak a berry into your mouth while the others are busy picking theirs.

Jan buys a big chest freezer for all the food. The only place it will fit is in front of the back door in the kitchen. That means you have to go out the front door and all the way around the house to get to the outhouse. I'm terrified when it's dark and I have to pee, and I try to get one of my brothers to go with me. If they won't, I sneak into the kitchen and find a cup to pee in. Mom and Jan don't see me, because they're usually drunk or asleep. I only got caught once, but that was because I chose a cup that was too small. I couldn't stop peeing when the cup filled up, so it ran out over my fingers and down in a thin stream, all the way to the door to the living room. Mom looked up and saw the river of pee. She ran over and helped me clean up. Jan never found out and Mom didn't yell at me.

I'm holding our puppy Bulder, from our German shepherd Tina's first litter. In addition to the two large dogs, we also had Sussi, a farm dog, and two cats, Mikkeline and Pelle. I was very attached to our animals, and when Jan mistreated them, I suffered just as much as when he beat my mother and brothers. Even when they were small pups, Jan would shove the dogs' snouts in their own feces or piss if they went indoors, and then lift them up by the nape and shake them as he screamed in their faces. If they bit him, he'd bite them back until they howled.

One day we find out that we're going to a community camp for summer vacation. We take the bus from Horslunde to Blåvandshuk to spend a week at a big place with dormitories. The adults at the camp play ball with us, and they take us down to the beach and out on evening field trips with flashlights. They also make delicious food, like ground beef with spaghetti, and mashed potatoes. And then we get dessert.

One morning the adults wake us up by saying "good night." I'm totally confused. Then they walk backward out the door. They tell us we all have to do it because today is "Backward Day." When we get to the dining room, there's ground meat with brown sauce on the tables. We have fun all day trying to do everything backward. It's really hard. You certainly can't start by drying yourself off first in the bathroom—just as you can't take food out of your mouth first when it's time to eat. It's the best day at camp.

Back home it turns out that I'm not the only one afraid to go out to the toilet at night. One morning when Jan is the first one out the front door, he comes running back in and screams: "Who the hell took a shit in front of the beech tree?" The beech tree is two yards from the front door. We stare at each other but don't say anything. The only thing I know is that it wasn't me.

He looks at all of us with dark, furious eyes and says: "You can all take your clothes off and go right back to bed. And you can lie there without any food until one of you remembers who did it. And when that person comes out and tells me, the rest of you can get up. The one who shit has to remove the crap with their bare hands."

I start to cry. I can see from his face that Michael is furious. Michael questions René and Tonny repeatedly, but both deny it. I don't know who to believe. We lie there for several hours, going back and forth between arguing and being silent. And then I have to pee, but I don't dare go out. Finally Tonny gets up, puts on his clothes, and goes outside to Jan and says it was him. He's told to remove the shit with his bare hands.

Tonny comes back in with Jan behind him. They go out into the hallway and then we hear the usual smacks and Tonny crying. Then Tonny goes back to bed without looking at the rest of us. Jan goes in after him and stays in the room for some time. They're whispering, and I can hear Jan breathing heavily. After that, Jan goes back into the garden. Meanwhile, Tonny has been told to stay in bed without talking to the rest of us.

In the evening, Tonny is allowed to come out and eat with us. We don't talk about what happened—but Mom and Jan are fighting more than they normally do. They're both drunk, and Jan sounds more malicious than usual. He accuses Mom of not being able to control her rotten kids, and she calls him a wuss who can't keep a job.

Suddenly Jan knocks over the coffee table. Then he jumps off the couch and grabs Mom around her neck with both hands. Her eyes get really wide, and she tries to say something but can't. We sit there silently listening to her wheeze. I feel as if I'm frozen in place and can't get up. Mom's face is getting redder and redder, her arms and legs are flying around, and she's kicked several things off the table.

Jan finally releases her, and she falls forward over the table. She lies there gasping for breath, all red in the face, saliva running out of her mouth. Jan wobbles away from the table, grabs his jacket in the hallway, and soon we hear his moped.

Still frozen, I sit and watch as my brothers help Mom up from the table. She gasps and cries and calls Jan a psychopath. Then she stands up to get a beer, and my brothers clear off the table. I'm terrified at the thought of Jan coming home again.

He doesn't come home before we go to bed. Once Mom has left the room, Tonny says: "I'm not the one who did it."

"No," says René, laughing. "It was me—but you gave up first."

In the morning, Jan is back home, and no one says anything about what happened the night before.

This picture was taken the summer Mom and Jan weren't drinking. We were allowed to go scouting and got these nice uniforms. We were going to scouting camp with Grethe Frost. I don't know why Tonny isn't in the picture—I believe he went scouting with us. In the background is a glimpse of our thatched house. Michael is on the left, René is to the right, and I'm in the middle.

Because of our problems going to the bathroom at night, Jan institutes a rule that we're not allowed to drink in the evening. Because then you have to pee. One night after we're tucked in, Tonny calls for Mom and asks if he can have some water. When Jan hears that, he comes to the doorway and says: "You can all get up and come out to the kitchen. Then Tonny can get some water." We walk out to the kitchen, where Jan fills a quart-size container with water. He tells Tonny: "Start drinking—and keep drinking until you throw up. If you empty the container, I'll fill it up again."

Tonny drinks. The rest of us don't say anything. I don't understand why Tonny can't just obey Jan's rules. Tears run down his cheeks while he drinks. Finally he starts making puking noises, and then he leans over the sink and throws up all the water. He dries his mouth off with a dishcloth, and then we all toddle off to bed.

After the episode when Jan almost strangled Mom, they both start to take Antabuse, a drug to treat their drinking. Everything gets calmer at home. They almost never argue or fight, and there's money for something other than alcohol and tobacco. Mom decides to get some mail-order clothes for us. We sit and look at catalogues, and I'm allowed to choose something. Most of the clothes I have look just like my brothers': T-shirts, shirts, and sweaters in dark colors, and corduroy or canvas pants. I inherited most of it from them, but Mom got some of it from a girlfriend.

I'm in first grade during that spring when they aren't drinking. The first warm spring day, Jan and Mom make a tent out of sheets in the backyard; they tie the sheets to some tree branches, so we can't see the sky. Then Jan makes a bonfire, and we bake twist bread and have a good time.

That spring, we're also allowed to go scouting, and Mom and Jan buy scouting uniforms for each of us. Grethe is my scoutmaster—she's also my gym teacher at school. Grethe has several troops, including some older girls, and sometimes she asks Mom and Jan if she can take me on their scouting trips. They always say yes, and I enjoy it.

Late that summer, Mom and Jan start drinking again, and the postman we've had since the day we moved to Lolland starts to come over.
He ends his route at our house and stays for hours every day. They sit
around drinking aquavit, beer, and homemade wine and listening to
records by Bjørn Tidmand, Gustav Winckler, Bjarne Liller, and John
Mogensen. On the days the postman comes, Mom and Jan don't come
out into the garden.

More and more frequently, we're home alone while Mom and Jan
are at a bar in Nakskov. We like being home alone, because we can do
what we're not allowed to when they're home. When there are eggs and
sugar, we make eggnog—if there are a lot of eggs, we each use two yolks.
My brothers aren't patient enough to wait until the eggnog is completely
mixed, so they eat the yolk while it's still dark yellow and the grains of
sugar still crunch. I'm the best mixer. I can keep at it until my eggnog
is all smooth and light yellow. When it's done, I lick the spoon. I can
spend several hours on eggnog.

One day we take our bikes to Hestehovedet, a beach that's roughly
ten miles away. I sit on the back of my brothers' bikes, and they take
turns giving me a ride there. When we finally reach the beach, my rear
end hurts and my brothers are tired. We run down to the water's edge
and jump into the water in just our underpants. It's low tide, so we can
go out pretty far. Michael and Tonny swim all the way out to where they
can't touch the bottom. I can't swim, so René and I stay in shallow water,
where we toss wet sand and jellyfish at each other. When we get tired of
swimming, we dry ourselves with our own clothes and then ride back
home. Along the way, we stop by some apple trees and eat a few apples.

We never know when Mom and Jan are coming home, but if they're
not there at dinnertime, we can usually find some bread or oatmeal.
One day there's nothing in the house. No oatmeal, no bread, no eggs,
no leftovers from the day before—just some margarine and milk in the
refrigerator. Finally Michael goes out to dig up some potatoes, which
he roasts for us. While he's making dinner, the telephone rings. It's Jan.

He asks Michael to find some money that's hidden, call for a taxi, and come into Nakskov with the money to get them. They owe some money at a bar, and it has to be paid before they can leave. Michael leaves in a taxi while the rest of us eat and clean up.

The fighting between Mom and Jan gets worse. One day when they're having one of their typical arguments about money, Jan stands up to get a beer in the kitchen. As he walks by, he smacks Mom in the back of the head and keeps going. Mom grabs a full glass ashtray and throws it at him. It hits him right in the back, the ashtray cutting him as it shatters. He turns around, pulls her up out of the chair, and slaps her head again. Mom head-butts him. Mom is proud of her head-butts. She once told me that she tore off a man's eyebrow by head-butting him. Jan pushes her away and runs out the back door yelling that he's going to get the axe so he can kill all of us.

Mom opens a window and we all jump out. I see Jan standing with the axe inside while we run as fast as we can over to Mom's friend Kirsten's. It's pitch-dark and we can't see where we're running. Terrified that he's going to come after us, I keep looking back, but it's hard to see in the dark. Once we get to Kirsten's house, Mom knocks on the door, and Kirsten lets us in. She's not surprised—she'd been married to a man who beat her.

Kirsten lets us sleep at her house. My brothers sleep in the loft with her children. Mom and I sleep in the living room with the dogs. The floor is covered with newspapers, and there must be at least ten dogs in the place. It stinks of dog food and dog shit, but that doesn't matter: the dogs are fun to play with and Kirsten is sweet. I like being there. The next day, Kirsten takes measurements so she can make me a dress. It will go all the way to the ground and have puffy sleeves—and she wants to sew me a little bag to go with it.

A few days later we go back to Nordlunde. Jan has bandages on both wrists, so I ask what happened. He says that he tried to commit suicide by slashing his arteries because he was tired of life, Mom, and us. When we're alone, my brothers talk about the different ways you can commit suicide. You can hang yourself, take pills, shoot yourself, cut yourself, or gas yourself. I become frightened. What are we going to do if Jan dies? Or Mom? I can't imagine life without them. Where would we live? From that day on, I get up at night while the others are sleeping to make sure the gas isn't on, and I check to see if the knives are where they should be. I'm afraid that Mom or Jan will kill us, themselves, or each other, so it gets harder and harder to sleep.

I also start to count. I repeat things in my head three times or in sets of three. When I'm playing, numbers whirl around inside my brain. The number of steps I'm taking, or even the number of times I open and close doors, becomes important. Every time I don't stick to the rule that everything has to happen in threes, I admonish myself that it has to be three times three the next time. If I screw up, I have to repeat it three times three times three. I know it's strange, so I don't tell anyone about it.

I include Mom in only one of my rituals. When we say good night, she has to say, "Good night," and then I answer, "Good night." Then she has to say, "Sleep tight," and I have to reply, "Thanks, you too." After that, she has to say, "Good night" again, and I have to answer, "Good night." If either one of us forgets even one of the words, I make her start all over again. She gets irritated with me when we have to start over, but she does it anyway.

My other grandma, Jan's mom, comes to visit a couple times a year, and we visit her sometimes too. She lives in an apartment on the island of Amager with a full bathroom with a toilet. Everything is squeaky clean and smells like strong soap. I like that smell. Grandma has short gray hair that's wavy, just like Jan's. She's usually wearing a newly ironed blouse, a smooth skirt that goes down to her knees, see-through stockings, and flat black shoes. I think she looks like a royal person in a movie. Tall and slender. I don't know how Jan can be her son.

Once when we were visiting her, she gave me a doll. She found it in a garbage can in the courtyard. She washed it with the same soap the apartment smelled like, and then sewed some new clothes for it. I was happy—a doll from Grandma that smelled like her.

Both Jan and Mom hate when Grandma comes to visit. They discuss it for a long time before she shows up, and they always end up arguing. Mom says that Jan is a wuss who lets his mother run his life. Jan replies that Mom can't keep a clean, nice house, so he's embarrassed when his mother comes. I know what Jan means. There's filth everywhere and large piles of dirty clothes, because Mom's always behind on the wash. It has to be done partly in the tub in the kitchen and partly in the big black pot for boiling water. Mom hates it.

When Grandma's here, Mom and Jan almost never drink. As soon as she arrives, Grandma starts cleaning and washing clothes. She also makes delicious food like meat loaf, veal patties, and other things we rarely get to eat. And she bakes cakes and bread, all of which is ready for us when we come home from school.

My brothers and I love when Grandma's here—even though we're a little afraid of her. Her eyes burn into us just like Jan's, and she's so tall she has to lean over when she talks to us. She usually stays for two weeks, or even longer, so we get used to her being here. She sleeps on a lounge chair in the living room and is the last to go to bed and the first to get up. And the mailman never stays to drink when Grandma's visiting.

One day when we come home from school, Mom and Jan are sitting there with the mailman, drinking again. We ask if we're going to get something to eat, which Grandma usually has ready for us. Jan laughs loudly and says: "The help just went home in a white taxi." Mom and the mailman laugh too. I can't understand why she never said goodbye.

1975–77

People in this town don't like us. When we go to the grocer's to sell empty bottles or buy beer, milk, or gasoline, he keeps an eye on us to see if we're stealing. I don't—but my brothers steal candy if they can get away with it. One day our cat Mikkeline comes home with a thick rubber band wrapped tightly around her neck; it has rubbed all the fur off and left a bloody circle. We're sure one of the neighbors did it.

When we aren't playing in the fields, we ride our bikes on the paths. My brothers decide to ride to a run-down farm a couple of miles from us. An old man holding a cat is standing out in the yard. He says hello and asks me if I'd like to have a cat. He says the cat just became a mother—and that there are a bunch of small kittens in the barn that we can look at. He shows us around the place. The barn is dilapidated, and it's clear that it's only being used as a home for the cats. There are old, dusty tractors and other pieces of farm equipment covered with spiderwebs. In one corner there are some old gray bales of hay where the cat had its kittens. She dug a hole in the hay, and six teeny kittens are meowing and crawling all over each other in there. The man says they have to get a little bigger before we can pick them up, but we can come and visit them whenever we want to.

He asks if we'd like to come in and have a soda. We walk through the kitchen, which smells like gas and old food. Dirty dishes are piled up on the kitchen table, and there's another small table with a yellow plastic tablecloth on it. Old newspapers cover half the table. He shows us into the living room, where the ceiling is much higher than in our house. It's dark, with thick curtains on the windows, dark flowered wallpaper, and dark wood furniture. There's a rack with pipes for smoking on the bookcase and a lot of old books. A thick layer of dust covers everything, and the whole place smells sweet and musty.

We sit around the dining room table. He gets four orange sodas for us, along with a beer for himself, and sits down at the end of the table. He asks us about everything—what our names are, where we live, and who our parents are. He says I have a fine name, Lisbeth, like in the song the comedian Dirch Passer sings. The old man starts to sing it: "There's a hole in the bucket, dear Lisbeth, dear Lisbeth; there's a hole in the bucket, dear Lisbeth, there's a hole." We laugh. He sounds just like Dirch Passer when he sings.

My brothers are all talking at the same time while I sit and stare at the man, whose name is Mogens. He lives alone but has grown children in Copenhagen. I slide down off my chair, walk over, and sit on his lap. He doesn't say anything; he just puts his arms around me while he keeps talking to my brothers. When we've finished our sodas, we have to get home to eat. He follows us out and says that we can come over whenever we want. We wave goodbye from our bikes and tell him we'll be back tomorrow.

We're having cabbage soup, so there aren't any glasses on the table. Jan says that there's enough water in the soup. We sit quietly and watch TV while we eat. It's the evening news. Now and then we look at each other, and I can tell that my brothers are also looking forward to visiting Mogens again. Suddenly Tonny says, "Mogens's cat has kittens."

Jan looks at Tonny in disbelief and yells: "Quiet while we're eating! Tonny, go to bed right now. I'm coming in there when I'm finished eating."

After we get home from school the next day, we rush over to see Mogens, who's standing at his kitchen window and waving at us. He opens the window and tells us we can go see the cats—and when we're ready, he's made some sandwiches for us. The kittens haven't gotten any bigger, so we can't pick them up. Still, we stick our fingers down into the hole in the bale of hay and pet them carefully.

Inside, Mogens has set out sodas and a large plate with sandwiches and a big blue plastic tub of strawberry jam on the table in the living room. While sitting on Mogens's lap, I eat till I'm ready to burst. I unbutton the top of my pants because my stomach hurts from eating too much. He puts his hand on the lowest part of my stomach, with his fingertips inside the top of my panties, while he slowly moves his fingers back and forth. My brothers can't see what he's doing with his hand. I think it feels nice to have a warm hand there.

Mogens asks if we like school. My brothers all say it's boring and the teachers are dumb, but I talk about all the things I've learned at school. I also tell him that I've been to the school psychologist. He asks me why, but I don't know—it was the school's idea. I had to put some puzzles together and look at some pictures and say what they reminded me of. It was really fun, and at the end the psychologist said that I was very clever and that I could go right into second grade instead of first. But Mom and Jan said no way, because I'd be two years younger than all the other children.

The only thing I don't like about school is that sometimes you have to go to the dentist. You walk over in a group, and they give you some red liquid you have to squish around in your mouth for two minutes before you can spit it out. Afterward you have to rinse your mouth out with water. If you've been brushing your teeth the right way at home, most of the red will disappear. If not, the red stays on your teeth. Then the dentist comes around to look at our teeth, and she always says that my parents aren't brushing my teeth well enough. Actually, they never brush them. The first time I went to the dentist, I had five cavities. When the dentist started drilling, I tried to get away, but two women held me down while yelling at me to sit still.

All the way home I'm afraid. I've eaten too much and I can't take another bite—and Jan will insist that I clean my plate.

We're going to have "fish hot dogs" with rye bread. Jan has cooked a big pot of hot dogs, which are now on the coffee table. It's called fish hot dogs because you have to use your fingers to fish up the hot dogs. At first the water is burning hot, so it hurts to grab the hot dogs. You can wait, but then you risk not getting many—the others will have already fished them up. Michael always gets the most, with Tonny and René fighting to be number two. That night, fish hot dogs are perfect for me, because I just wait till the water cools off and then only fish up one hot dog.

It soon becomes a tradition to visit Mogens after school and on the weekends. I always stay close to him while my brothers run around. Mogens tells them to play outdoors and lets them do whatever they want out there. He has a big garden of fruit trees, and they can eat as much as they want. They can saw off branches too, and they spend a lot of time playing Tarzan out there. Michael is Tarzan—and he teases the other two by saying Tonny is the ape and René is Jane.

Mogens and I spend most of the time indoors. What I like best is sitting on his lap and talking. My pants or shorts are always open, and he usually has his hand in my panties, so that his fingertips are gently touching the top of my pee-pee. Whenever he hears the boys come in, he quickly pulls out his hand.

One day I tell him I have to pee and hop off his lap. He says he wants to help me, so we go to the bathroom together. It's dirty but not half as dirty as our outhouse. I pull down my shorts and sit on the toilet. Mogens crouches down in front of me, pulls my pants and underpants all the way down to the floor, and spreads my legs a little more. He sticks one of his index fingers between my thighs, inside my pee-pee, and slowly moves it back and forth. He's breathing heavy as he asks if I like it. "Yes," I say, though I'm not sure what he means. I sit quietly waiting for him to stop, but he keeps doing it. Finally I tell him I can't pee when he does that and when he's in the room. Then he stops and says he'll be waiting right outside the door and that I can call after I've peed, so he can help me with my pants.

After I've peed, I pull up my pants by myself. I walk over to the mirror and look at myself for a while. I don't look in a mirror that often. There's a small one at home in the kitchen. It hangs so high on the wall that I have to stand on a chair to look into it. Mogens's mirror is big. My short hair is light and messy. Mom calls the dirt on my neck "ring around the collar." My nails are black, my hands are full of warts, and my eyes are red and inflamed. And I have eczema on my elbows. I'm ugly. I wash my hands with soap that has "LUX" written on it. It smells wonderful.

I walk out. Mogens, who's standing right by the door, looks disappointed.

"You were supposed to call," he says.

"Yeah, but I could pull up my own pants," I say as I walk by him.

He grabs my arms and says he wants to tickle me. He carries me over to the bed, where he throws me down and then sits on top of me while tickling me. I squeal with laughter. He keeps doing it until finally, out of breath, he tosses himself onto the bed next to me.

He says he wants to show me something that will tickle in a different way. He sits up, pushes himself farther down the bed, and lies down again with his lips against my thighs. He starts kissing them carefully while I chuckle. Then I can feel his tongue up under my shorts, which he's trying to push up with one hand. I lie completely still. It feels nice.

Suddenly someone is pounding on the window, and I hear loud laughter from outside. My brothers have been standing there watching what we're doing. Mogens jumps up, straightens out his clothes, and says that we have to go home now. I stand up and, confused, race out into the courtyard. Mogens shuts the door behind me before I even get to say goodbye.

My brothers say they saw him touching me—and now they're going to tell Mom and Jan about it. I feel ashamed, and I'm afraid Jan will punish me for it.

When we get home, I tiptoe into the living room. Michael dashes out into the garden and tells Mom and Jan that Mogens is an old pig who was fondling me. Mom calls for me to come out. They don't yell at me, but we're told we can never go over there again. Mom and Jan have a discussion about what they should do and if they should go to the police. "That won't do any good," says Jan. "But we'll tell everyone what he's done."

The next time the postman shows up, Mom and Jan tell him about that bastard on that farm who fondled me. I go outside to pet the cats. It's all so embarrassing.

Sometime later, I'm sitting on the back of Michael's bike as we ride by the farm. We can see children running around in the garden and that the house has been painted. We ride our bikes up to the house. A man and woman are standing together and talking in the courtyard. Michael asks where Mogens is.

"He's moved," says the man.

A girl about my age runs over and asks if we'd like to try her swing set. I'd really like to, so I hop off the bike. It's over in the garden where a bunch of the trees my brothers were playing in have been chopped down. We swing until the man comes over and says that Louise can't play anymore.

The next day we ride back up there and knock on the door. The man comes out and says we can't run over here all the time. We ride back home and decide that these people are snobs and we don't want to go there again.

Dad and Anita visit a couple of times. One day they come to take us with them on a summer vacation. They've moved to a brand-new house in Køge, and now we have two half brothers, Tommy and Kenneth. They aren't in the car—someone's watching them while Dad and Anita come to Lolland to get us.

When I'm at their house in Køge, it's like being in another world. There's no smell of cigarettes. Instead, I smell coffee, leather, paint, wood, and Anita's perfume. The one-story house is white brick, and there's a garden all around it with newly planted grass. We're not allowed to walk on the short green grass until it's done growing, but there's a patio we can go out on. There are three bedrooms and a big bathroom with a toilet and bathtub. The walls are bright and there are green plants everywhere.

I love my new little brothers. They're three and five, blond as can be, and unbelievably sweet. Kenneth, the oldest, is very timid, whereas Tommy is always running around and making noise. I get to sleep in their room, while they sleep with Dad and Anita. My big brothers will be in the guest bedroom, which has a pullout bed.

There's an organ in the living room, along with a color TV and some black leather furniture. It's a Hammond organ, which Dad plays—and I'm allowed to play it too (with the headphones on). I can sit there for hours making sounds and rhythms by pressing the keys. Dad can play Shu-bi-dua's "Chicken and Ice Cream and Hot Dogs" and a lot of other songs. And he's a good singer.

One day while we're eating, we start talking about what we're learning in school. I mention that I can spell anything because I never make mistakes in dictation. I'm in second grade. Dad asks if I'm sure about that. "Yes," I say. "Just give me a word to spell." Standing up to get a piece of paper and a pen, he asks me to write the word "station." That's not hard, I think. I write "stasion" and hand him the paper. He roars with laughter and says it's wrong. I stare down at my plate and keep eating, wondering why I haven't learned how to spell that word.

Anita is good to us. She makes ice cream sundaes: she puts scoops of vanilla ice cream in a tall glass and then pours chocolate syrup over it and adds whipped cream on top. We each get a glass with a straw and a spoon. She also wants to take me to the hairdresser. I've never been—Mom usually cuts our hair. So one day while we're visiting them, Anita and I drive to the hairdresser in their white Volkswagen. Anita sits down with the other women who are waiting and reads a ladies' magazine. The hairdresser wets my hair and starts combing it. Suddenly she stops, looks down at my scalp, and yells: "She's full of lice!" She looks over at Anita. "Look at this. Her whole scalp is alive with them. I can't cut her hair."

I sit completely still and stare in the mirror at the two of them discussing my lice. Anita says that we'll have to go home but that first we'll stop at the drugstore to buy some lice treatment.

As soon as we walk in the door to the house, Anita announces that she's never been so embarrassed. My brothers and I are all deloused, and we get new clothes too.

In the car on the way home from summer vacation, I ask Dad and Anita why they don't visit us more often. Dad says that they've tried but that Mom and Jan hide us when they're coming. When we get home, we wave goodbye and go in to Mom and Jan. I'd rather be with Dad and Anita.

Mom and Jan start spending more time at bars in Nakskov, especially one near the train station—the Iron Rod. Sometimes they take us with them. The Iron Rod is separated into two sections: one is a little nicer than the other. The tables have tablecloths on them, and the room is bright with large windows facing the train station. If you walk through an arch, you enter a bar with tall barstools. Next to the bar is another room where you can play pool. Mom loves to play pool—and she often wins. The people are nice and they give us money for candy and the one-armed bandit. I like to sit and play that while eating a grilled cheese sandwich. Sometimes we walk over to the restaurant in the train station, which is right across from the Iron Rod, and then I get tomato soup with fish meatballs. Usually, though, I eat grilled cheese if I'm hungry—and I get a Coke with it.

One day when I'm alone with Mom and Jan at the bar, they start to fight. Jan grabs Mom by the hair, pulls her off the barstool, and drags her to the entrance; he opens the door and throws her out onto the street. He yells at me to go out with my fucking mother. I don't want to, because I'm playing the one-armed bandit. The bartender yells that children can't be there without their parents. Jan is sitting on a barstool with his back turned toward me.

Crying, I walk out onto the street, where Mom is waiting. Right at that moment, my gym teacher, Grethe, comes by. When I see her, I start crying loudly and say, "Take me home with you, Grethe."

"Lisbeth, you know I can't do that," she says.

"Take the little bastard with you," says Mom as she shoves me toward Grethe.

Grethe takes my hand and we walk off together.

1977–78

Grethe takes me home to her husband, Otto. They have three children, but only their son René still lives at home. René is a few years older than me. Grethe drives to my house in Nordlunde to get me some clothes and my schoolbag. Meanwhile, I stay with Otto, who gives me some juice and butters some rolls for me. He looks at me while I'm eating, and then he grabs both my arms and twists them around so my forearms are facing up.

"What are these on your arms?" he asks.

I have a lot of marks on my arms.

"I don't know," I say.

When Grethe returns, she has my schoolbag with her. She couldn't find any clothes worth taking. Grethe says that our home is no place for people to be living. "There's a mess all over the kitchen," she says, shaking her head. She's going to the township tomorrow to see what can be done. Otto shows her the marks on my arms, and they say they look like cigarette burns.

"Are you sure you can't remember how you got them?" asks Grethe.

"Yes," I reply.

Grethe and Otto live in a big two-story house in Lindet, just outside of Nakskov. It's a small town with just a couple of houses and a tiny train station where the train—or "the pig," as we call it—to Nakskov stops, but only if you push a button by the tracks.

On the first floor, there's a large kitchen and a gigantic living room with carpets and enough room for a dining room table and sofas in front of a color TV. We usually sit here at night and watch TV while Grethe and Otto have coffee. René and I get juice. I have my own small room on the second floor; it's normally used as a guest room. There's a bed, a dresser for my clothes, a small desk, and a bookcase. When I'm sitting at the desk, I can look over at the train tracks.

There's a small lamp hanging over my bed. I'm afraid to sleep alone, so the light has to stay on all night. One night I wake up because something is burning my thigh. The lamp is resting on it—the shade is gone and the bulb is burning my skin. There's a large bright-red mark on my thigh and a large black hole in the foam mattress. I jump out of bed and try to hang the lamp back up, but the screw is gone and I don't know what I should do. I take the lamp with me and step out into the hall, where I start to cry. I don't go downstairs to Grethe and Otto, who are sleeping. I just stand there crying, not knowing what to do. Grethe and Otto come running upstairs. Grethe holds and comforts me while she looks at my thigh. We go down to the kitchen, where I'm given a wet cloth to put on my thigh and a glass of milk. Meanwhile, Otto fixes the lamp so I can go back to sleep. From that day on, I turn off the lamp by unplugging it, even though I'm afraid of the dark. Grethe keeps the light on in the hall and the door to my room open wide. I check the lamp at least three times before I go to sleep each night. If I do it wrong, I have to do it all again, three times three times three.

My days spent with Grethe and Otto are all alike. I ride with Grethe to school and then back home again. Grethe also takes me to Girl Scouts, and I go with them when they visit family and friends. I like being with them, but I'm also a little intimidated by them. One day they tell me we're going on a vacation in Jutland to visit some of Grethe and Otto's friends and stay at a campsite. René and I play with the other children at the campground. We're there for a week, and the time goes by quickly.

The day after we get home, someone knocks on the door. Outside there's a woman from the township, along with a policeman. They say I have to go with them and that Grethe and Otto need to pack my things. Grethe yells at them, but Otto is completely silent. The woman says the police are here because Grethe and Otto wouldn't turn me over, as Mom said they had to. I don't cry. I'm frozen in place, just like that time Jan almost strangled Mom. I've been living with Grethe and Otto for half a year now, and I've only seen my mother one single Sunday afternoon.

The woman and the policeman drive me to the orphanage in Nakskov. In the evening I'm tucked in by Frederiksen, a sweet old lady with big, soft lips. She smells like cigars. I cry quietly in my bed. I'm not afraid; I'm just sad. Why couldn't I stay with Grethe and Otto? It would have made more sense if I had to go home to be with Mom—but why did they have to put me in an orphanage?

The orphanage is on the outskirts of Nakskov. My section faces the playground where there are swings and large red tricycles that are fun to ride. The orphanage also has two horses you can ride. I really like the horses, but I'm afraid to fall off, although there's always an adult holding on to the horse. So I only try that a couple of times. Still, I often go out to talk to them when they're in the pen, and I give them grass and dandelions. The pen is close to the playground, so I'm not afraid. On the other hand, I don't like walking farther out, because I am afraid of the big kids at the orphanage.

I've changed schools now. Byskolen is a big redbrick school with a lot of floors, and it has a slanted roof running all along the schoolyard. None of the others from my section of the orphanage go to that school, so every day I ride there alone on one of the orphanage's bikes. That doesn't bother me. In general, I like to ride by myself in Nakskov. The road to the school goes right past the Iron Rod, and now and then I stop in the afternoon to see if Mom and Jan are there. Sometimes I get lucky—and then they give me money and buy me a soda and a grilled cheese sandwich.

In school, you have to go outside for recess. I keep to myself, close to the entrance beneath the slanted roof, so I can get to class quickly when the bell rings. At lunch, they open a window beneath the roof where you can buy a small rye bread sandwich with cheese. Whenever I have the money, I buy one. We get an allowance at the orphanage; I use the money I don't spend on candy on bread and cheese. Sometimes I get some money from Mom and Jan too.

RAVNSBORGSKOLEN
4913 HORSLUNDE
TELEFON (03) 93 51 76

KOPI

Den 9. august 1977

Ref.:

Socialforvaltningen
Ravnsborg Rådhus
4913 Horslunde

Jeg har d.d. modtaget skrivelse fra Socialforvaltningen
vedr. elev Lisbeth Malene Zornig Andersen - (indskrevet under
efternavn: Nygaard).

Jeg forstår skrivelsen således:
I) Socialudvalget har flyttet eleven fra familiepleje
hos Grethe Frost til institutionen: Børne- og ungdomscentret
i Nakskov.

II) Den sidste linie i skrivelsen skal formodentlig for-
stås således, at man anmoder om at få eleven udskrevet fra Ravnsborgskolen til fortsat skolegang på Byskolen i Nakskov.

Skrivelsen har været forevist klasselærer - lærerråds-
formand og faglærere og Socialudvalgets beslutning har været drøf-
tet.

Der er fuld enighed om, at eleven i den tid, hun har været i familiepleje, har været fuldstændig i balance, glad og til-
freds samt ren og velplejet. Hendes udbytte af skolegangen har
derfor været særdeles godt og gode fremskridt er konstateret. Hun
har ligeledes været fuldt accepteret blandt kammerater. Der er
for os ingen tvivl om, at alle disse ting i væsentlig grad skyl-
des, at hun har været i et hjem, hvor man virkelig gjorde noget
for hende og holdt af hende, hvilket hun også selv har givet ud-
tryk for

Vi er derfor nærmest rystede over Socialudvalgets dispo-
sition, hvor en afgørelse om en elev er truffet, uden at man har
indhentet oplysninger fra skolen. Det lover ikke godt for et evt.
fremtidigt samarbejde mellem skole og Socialforvaltning.

Vi finder afgørelsen helt forkert, idet man slet ikke kan
have taget hensyn til, hvad der i dette tilfælde er bedst for barnet. Netop i dette tilfælde finder vi, at en anbringelse på institution ikke kan være så godt for barnet som en privat pleje, hvor
barnet oplever et familiefællesskab og finder den tryghed, der
kan være i noget sådant.

kopi til Skoleforvaltning.
. . Skolenævn.

---

*I found this letter of protest in my case files. In it, a group of my teachers fight for me to remain
with Otto and Grethe. I was deeply touched when I read it. Later I met with Randi, my homeroom
teacher from that time, who told me she had been quite fond of me. I also met with my math teacher,
Stig Vestergaard, who later became mayor of Lolland township. Before I gained access to my files—
and spoke to Randi, Stig, Grethe, and Otto—I was very critical about whether foster care was good
for me. Until then, I had thought that I was too troubled to be placed with a family. After researching
this book, however, I realized that this view had nothing to do with reality: I had based my adult
rationalizations about foster families versus twenty-four-hour care on my painful separation from
Otto and Grethe. I had repressed most of my time with them—repressed the fact that, actually, I had
repeatedly insisted on returning to foster care. All of this has emerged as both warm and heartrending
memories from my childhood when, after I was removed, no one was listening to me.*

After a month at the orphanage, I have to go home to live with Mom. I don't understand why I had to leave Grethe and Otto and go to the orphanage—and now why I have to live with Mom and change schools all over again. No one explains anything to me.

Mom and Jan are divorced now. My brothers don't live at home anymore, and Mom and I move to a small row house in Torrig. Torrig is nothing more than a few houses along the main road. We live a hundred yards inside the town limits. To me, it's like living out in the country. The cars seem to think so too. They drive really fast, and one day the mother and grandmother of Brian, who's in my class, miss a curve and die. Our teacher tells us about it the next day. A few days later, Brian comes back to school. No one says anything, not even Brian. Not that I wish Brian well—but losing your mother and grandmother is the worst thing I can imagine.

Brian is one of my tormentors. Actually, he's the only one who really teases me. The others just watch. Brian says I smell and my clothes are ugly. I try to remember to take a bath. I just don't like to, because you can't lock the door to the shared bath where my mother and I live. So I rush through it every second or third day—and sometimes every fourth.

On my way to school, I cycle through all of Torrig and on to Birket, a slightly larger town with a school. I often have a stomachache. When I ride home after school, I usually have to stop somewhere between the signs for Torrig and Birket to squat down until my stomachache passes. That usually helps. Maybe I can't tolerate the yogurt we get every day at school, but I don't say anything because I love it. If I'm lucky, I get peach melba. An entire lunch hour can pass from when I slowly tear off the lid to when the container is empty and licked completely clean.

The house in Torrig belongs to the township—it's for people who can't afford to buy their own home. All the row houses have a teeny garden, and the toilets are outside; the outhouses are lined up in a row in the backyard with a number on each door. Even though the doors aren't locked, we never use each other's toilets. And there are shared baths.

Our house consists of a living room, a kitchen, a pantry, a bedroom, and an extra room outside next to the shared bath. The extra room can't be locked, so if you want to, you can enter it directly from outside. That room is mine—but I dare not sleep there. What if someone came into the room in the middle of the night?

At first Mom insists that I sleep there, but I just lie awake every night. I usually end up sneaking back into the apartment during the night and lying down next to Mom in her double bed, or else I sleep on the sofa. I'm only allowed to sleep in Mom's bed when she doesn't get home before I go to sleep. Jan thinks it's a shame, though, so he convinces Mom to let me sleep there all night, whether she's home or not. Even though Mom and Jan are divorced—and Mom sees other men—he still comes over.

When I go to bed on those nights Mom doesn't come home, I lie awake listening for cars and mopeds. I learn the sound of her boy-friends' cars and mopeds, because that means she's home. And I can always recognize Jan's moped.

The living room is twice as big as the one we had in Nordlunde, and Mom uses the money she gets from the township to buy furniture. We have a three-piece sofa set and a round brown dining room table with matching chairs. I don't really know why she wants that dining room table: we're still eating on the sofa with the TV on.

Mom was very beautiful as a young woman. I love this passport photo of her—she looks happy and confident.

The kitchen is also large and has yellowish wallpaper, a dark-green gas stove, and a checkered carpet in shades of dark green. Near the stove, the carpet is spotted and shiny, but Mom just loves that carpet. "It's so nice to have carpeting in the kitchen," she says. The kitchen has a really small pantry that's painted white and a small window too, so there's really nice light in there. I really like that room and I keep it nice and neat.

You can never predict the days in Torrig. Sometimes it's peaceful with just Mom and me in the apartment or with the TV on. Mom doesn't work, but I have to get up and go to school every day. Now and then she gets up to see me off, but when she sleeps in because she came home late the night before, I get up, put on my clothes, butter a piece of rye bread and add sugar, drink a glass of milk, and rush off on my bike.

When I come home from school and Mom's there, we watch TV or go to the laundromat. It's cozy in there—and the clothes always smell so nice afterward. After so many years of washing them by hand, Mom loves to wash clothes at the laundromat. But it's expensive. Otherwise I pass the days doing my homework or playing in the garden. If it snows, I try to build an igloo or dig snow caves; in the summer, I build huts and holes out of branches.

It's not so peaceful when Mom has guests or my brothers are home for the weekend. I tend to stay in the room out back or in the garden. I prefer being where it's not crowded with other people. I used to run all over with my brothers, but I've weaned myself off doing that—in fact, now it almost irritates me. They're always fighting with each other and with Mom. And when Jan's there, things can really explode. So I go for a walk.

Jan's not as tough anymore. You can really tell that he's only visiting, and both Mom and he try to maintain a good mood when my brothers are home. They've grown too, so Jan is a little more cautious about hitting them. Oddly enough, lately it's Mom who's been hitting my brothers more. She really flips out at Michael. One day Michael says something that compels Mom to grab a hanger and start beating him with it. He crawls into a ball on the kitchen floor as she keeps slamming the hanger onto his back. Suddenly the hanger breaks. Mom tosses it aside, grabs Michael by the hair, drags him to the front door, throws him out, and locks the door. Michael knocks hard on the door for a while, but finally he gives up and starts walking around the house and looking in the windows. Mom goes into the bedroom and shuts the door behind her. I think she's crying.

I was standing in the living room watching, surprised Mom was hitting him so hard—and with a hanger. She's never done that before, nor has she ever locked anyone out. I'm also surprised Michael wasn't hitting back. He just took it without defending himself or crying. I walk over and unlock the door, and after a little while Michael comes back. We don't talk about it. I think Michael is ashamed.

All four of us are at home for the first Christmas in Torrig. Jan is also there on Christmas Eve. Everyone enjoys the excellent roast pork and brown sauce Mom's made. She can't really make anything else that tastes as good as her roast pork—except pancakes, which she can flip into the air. One day she tosses the pan so high that one of the pancakes sticks to the ceiling. We all laugh about it for a long time. It's funny about Mom: Most of the time I get the feeling she's in her own world with no regard for us. Yet sometimes, like that day with the pancakes, she's fun and foolish like a real mother. At these times she calls me "Mouse."

This Christmas we have a tree, just a small one in a corner of the living room, and Mom has woven some paper hearts and bought a star. Mom is really good with her hands. She can draw the sweetest babies, and she can weave Christmas hearts and fold napkins till they look like something you'd see in a restaurant. She says she learned how to do it as a waitress.

There are gifts for all of us beneath the tree, but I got one in advance: a desk that's been set up for me in the living room. It's dark brown and has a red chair that goes with it. I'm happy. I can do my homework and sit and draw there. On Christmas Eve, I get a Disney writing pad and a blue Disney trash can. Now I have a desk—just like Natacha in my class. Natacha is an only child who has beautiful long dark hair that's always braided; she has a typewriter, her own room, a horse, two parents who are teachers, and a grandmother who lives next door.

We eat in silence. My brothers and I wash up, and then we open gifts. We don't do the traditional dance around the Christmas tree in our home. Then we all watch TV for the rest of the night. There's always a lot of good TV on Christmas Eve.

The next day we celebrate Christmas with herring, beer, and aquavit. Alfred next door and some of his friends are there too. We children eat quickly and disappear. My brothers roam the neighborhood. I keep to my room out back, where I lie reading. I'm into the Puk books.

After Christmas, Mom starts acting strangely. Sometimes she has seizures and falls down unconscious. She lies on the floor until she wakes up, and then she stands up and acts like nothing has happened. She also starts threatening to commit suicide. She always makes these threats while Jan's there and they're drunk. One afternoon, she explains in great detail how she's going to kill herself. She's going to slash her wrists, but first she'll turn on the gas in case she doesn't bleed to death.

Mom describes her plan while she and Jan are sitting on the living room sofas, with empty bottles and full ashtrays all over the table. Jan just laughs and says he's looking forward to it—then he can finally get some peace. I take my usual walk along the fields to try to calm down. I can't concentrate on my reading, because I'm more worried than I usually am and have to count all the time. I count trees, cars, and houses—and then I count combinations of all three things. Thoughts of my mother keep distracting me. There are too many details in her suicide plan. I think she might just do it. So I decide to remove all the razor blades and knives when I can do so without her finding out.

When I get back home, I sneak out into the kitchen and put all the knives—except the butter knives—in a trash bag, along with the razor blades. I take the bag and a spoon out to the backyard. It's dark. I find a spot where I can dig, and even though it's freezing outside, I manage to dig a small hole with the spoon. I put the bag down there and then quickly cover the hole and hurry back in.

I stay awake until I'm sure Mom and Jan are sleeping and then check the gas. Nothing else happens that night. Mom and Jan fall asleep, each on their own sofa. I turn off the lights, lock up, and go to bed. Sometime at night, they wake up and come into bed with me. I get up and check the gas again. The next morning I run out to find the knives before Jan and Mom wake up—but I can't find them. In the course of the day, Mom asks where all the knives are.

"I hid them because you said you wanted to commit suicide yesterday, and now I can't find them," I reply.

"Okay," says Mom.

A few days later she buys a new set.

For a while Jan comes over so often that I'm not sure he hasn't moved in. He says he still has the house in Nordlunde. I feel unsafe when he's there and just wish he'd go back home, which he does now and then, but sometimes he stays overnight. When he's there, the three of us sleep together in the double bed. I lie on the edge by the window, Jan in the middle, and Mom on the other side. I make every effort to lie as far over as possible so I don't have to touch Jan. I think he's disgusting with his big hair, full red beard, black teeth, and hairy, freckled back.

Every time Jan sleeps over, he and Mom have sex, unless they're both drunk and have been fighting or have fallen asleep in the living room. I act like I'm asleep when they're having sex, even though their violent movements make me bounce up and down in bed.

I start to suffer from back pain, which I try to alleviate by putting the comforter and mattress from my doll carriage on top of the sheet to make the bed feel a little softer. On the days when I have a stomachache and back pain, the bike ride home from school can really hurt. At the same time, I'm having trouble breathing because of my asthmatic bronchitis. Twice within a short period of time, I've had polyps in my nose removed because I can only breathe through my mouth.

One night while Jan and Mom are having sex again, I ask: "What are you doing?" Of course I know what they're doing—I don't really know why I ask. They're silent for a long time, and then Jan says: "We're doing something that feels really good. Try touching your privates, so you can see how nice it feels." I try it, but I don't think it feels that nice. I liked it better when Mogens was touching me. They go on having sex, and I go to sleep.

The next night, Jan's there again. They put Teddy Bear's Friends on the stereo, and there's a bottle of cherry wine on the coffee table. They call me in and ask if I'd like to try a little cherry wine. It's sweet and tastes like cherries, they tell me, and when you drink it, you'll feel nice and relaxed all over. I'm ten years old and have never tried alcohol before. "Okay," I say, sitting down with them.

It's sweet—but there's a strong taste of alcohol too. I don't really like it, but it's not totally disgusting. I drink all of it, and then Jan pours another. After I drink the second glass, I can feel my body starting to buzz. Jan gives me a third. He seems excited, although Mom looks nervous. I'm happy to see Jan in a good mood, and before long I'm singing with the music and dancing around the living room with Jan.

Suddenly he says: "Well, it's about time to go to bed. Lisbeth, why don't you take a bath before you go to bed?" I'm confused and my head is swimming—but I'm starting to grasp what's about to happen. It has something to do with what happened last night. I take a bath, put on some clean underwear, and go to bed. Mom and Jan are still sitting in the living room. A little later they come into the bedroom. I've turned off the light, and I'm lying with my back to the middle and pretending I'm asleep. They take their clothes off and crawl under their comforter. They start having sex, but suddenly it's quiet. I feel my comforter slowly being pulled off me. Jan crawls down to the end of the bed. He pulls off my panties, spreads my legs, and lies down between them. I don't resist. He starts gently moving his tongue around in my privates while caressing my thighs. At one point he lies across the bed so he can stick his penis inside Mom while he continues moving his tongue around. I can't hear Mom's breathing—only Jan's, which gets louder and louder. Suddenly he moves away, gets up on his knees, grabs Mom's rear end, and lifts her up on all fours; he pumps hard into her, back and forth, while roaring loudly. Afterward, he plops down in the middle of the bed and falls asleep in a few seconds.

I lie with my back to Mom and Jan and try to sleep, but it's impossible. I don't know where my panties are—and I don't dare turn the light on to find them.

The next day we act like nothing happened. I keep watching Mom to see if she's angry with me. She seems unfazed. Maybe she was so drunk that she can't remember anything. I hope so. I'm terribly frightened. I know what happened last night is totally wrong, and I'm ashamed I didn't resist.

1979–80

It's summer vacation. For the last few years, my brothers and I have gone to camp, but this year I'm not doing anything. Maybe we'll visit Grandma and Grandpa in Copenhagen, or maybe I'll go stay with Dad and Anita.

There's a two-story, green, wooden house with a large garden next to our row home, and a married couple in their fifties moves in with a big black Labrador. While they're emptying the moving van, the dog is running all over the garden. As I walk toward the hedge, it sprints over to me with its tongue hanging out because it wants to be petted. There's a tag on its collar: "Troll." Good name!

I say hello to Troll every day when I see him outside. He looks for me too, and I always laugh a lot when he comes galloping toward me. He's way too fat—just like his mother, the lady of the house. The husband isn't quite so fat.

One day while I'm talking to Troll, the husband comes over and asks my name.

"Lisbeth," I reply.

"My name's Holst. I'm going to be teaching at Birket School after summer vacation," he says. "Do you go there?"

"Yes," I answer.

"You're welcome to come into the garden anytime and play with Troll," Holst says.

I'd like that. Actually, I'd really like to take Troll for a walk, but I think he's too strong for me, and I don't want to ask. All summer long, Holst—who has a lot of wild black hair with a bald spot in the middle, a mustache, and big, bushy eyebrows—takes care of the garden while puffing on his pipe. He plants flower beds, edges and seeds the lawn, and burns yard waste. I follow after him with Troll, and he tells me everything about roses and burning off your garden.

Sometimes Ragna, Holst's wife, comes out into the garden to talk. A small, round, happy lady with pretty upswept hair, she wears a lot of makeup. You can trace the edge of powder all around her face, and her bright lipstick runs off a little into the wrinkles around her mouth. You can really see it when she smokes her cigarettes, Vikings. They're unbelievably strong—much stronger than the cigarettes Mom and Jan roll at home—but I like the smell when it mixes with Holst's pipe tobacco. One day when Ragna comes out into the garden to call Holst in for lunch, she asks if I'd like to come in and eat with them. Ragna calls Holst "Hans-Peder." I just say Holst.

Inside there are bookshelves everywhere, and they're crammed full of books and knickknacks. Paintings of animals and landscapes hang all over the walls. There's a small open kitchen with some kind of counter and a small breakfast nook on the other side of the counter. The table has been set with three place mats, teacups, and small lunch plates. I've never seen place mats before. The door to one room is open, so I can see that it's Holst's office. It's also full of books, and in the middle of it all there's a large dark-wood desk with a typewriter on it. I can't stop looking at it, so Holst asks if I'd like to write something on it.

"Yes," I say.

"You may—after we've eaten," he says.

There's rye bread and white bread, and on the table, there are different cold cuts you can choose. And there are sliced cucumbers and tomatoes, raw and fried onions, remoulade, and a bunch of other things. Ragna also makes chocolate milk for me: she mixes chocolate powder from a yellow packet and cold milk. Do she and Holst drink chocolate milk this way—or did they buy it just for me?

After we've eaten, Holst asks if I'd still like to write on his type-writer. "Yes!" I almost yell. We go into his office, where he shows me how to put paper in the typewriter and change lines. I tried Natacha's typewriter once, briefly, but this one is much bigger and does a lot of things I've never seen before. He walks out, sits down in his easy chair, lights his pipe, and starts to read the newspaper.

I start to type. At first I just want to try all the letters, but then I try to see how fast I can type. Suddenly all the keys get stuck in the middle. Now I've destroyed it. My heart is pounding so hard that I can hear it. I look into the living room. Holst is sitting with the newspaper on his lap and his head leaning back against the easy chair's headrest, his mouth open and his eyes closed. Meanwhile, Ragna is rummaging around in the kitchen. Carefully, I try to untangle the keys, one by one, and it works.

I start typing actual words. I take a book off the shelves. A hymnal. I copy "Lo, How a Rose E'er Blooming" on the typewriter. Suddenly I realize that Holst is standing in the doorway. He bends over to see what I've written. "You're very good," he says. I only copied it, but it makes me happy anyway. He leaves the room, and I hear him putting on his shoes to go back out into the garden. I grab my sheet of paper and go out after him.

It soon becomes a tradition to go over to Holst's to eat and write on his typewriter. One day they tell me that Mom has asked if they could watch me at night now and then—and they've said yes. I get a room on the second floor, where there are two rooms and another living room. I have to sleep on a sofa bed, which is soft and good for my back.

The first time I sleep over, we watch the news together. I'm not really interested, and anyway I have my own book to read. I saw *The*

Fishermen on television and then found out the film was based on a book, which I borrowed from the school library. So, I've been reading that. There's another book called *The Day Laborers*, and I'm going to read that one next. Reading *The Fishermen* puts me in the same mood as when I saw *Ditte, Child of Man*. I cried at all the evil things Ditte had to go through, yet at the same time I was happy that my own life is so much better. We're poor too, but no one is so mean to us.

The first night I sleep at Holst's house, I wake up because I have to pee. I can hear that Holst and Ragna have gone to bed. I get up, and just as I'm about to take my first step to go downstairs, I see a figure walk by in a big white dress, with three or four long, thin gray wisps of hair on her head. I freeze with terror. It's a ghost on its way into Holst's bedroom. Suddenly the figure says something—but it's Ragna's voice! Is this how Ragna looks at night? What happened to the hair she has during the day?

Kan du se den fugl
den flyver i skjul
den bange blif
når os den ser.

Kan du se det lam
det ligner ham
du ved ham med krøllerne
der er sammen med bøllerne

Kan du se alt sammen
det er til fryd og gammen
Gud skaber alt ,
det har Jesus fortalt

I used to love to type on Holst's typewriter, especially poems. This is a poem I wrote. It reads: "Can you see that bird / Hiding as it flies / Filled with fear / When it sees us near. / Can you see that lamb / It's just like him / With the hair that's curly / Hanging with the bullies. / Can you see everything / Created for joy / God creates everything / As Jesus said." At this point in our time in Torrig, I was preoccupied with faith. I turned our pantry into a prayer room. As an adult, I talk a great deal with my children about faith and whether God exists. I still have doubts. You can see the thumbtack holes in the plastic around the poem. Until I became an adult, I had it hanging in my room—wherever I lived.

The next morning, I look at Ragna in a whole new light. She wears a wig and has to be picked up in an ambulance once a week. I wonder if she's sick. What will happen to Holst and Troll if Ragna dies? Holst isn't very good in the kitchen.

One day I come over to Holst's to eat and have chocolate milk, as usual, but Ragna isn't home and Holst seems confused. I help him find food in the refrigerator and set the table. At one point, he says: "Oh yes, we need to make some chocolate milk for you." He grabs the brown package of chocolate instead of the yellow one and puts a teaspoonful in a glass. I know it's wrong, but I don't say anything. He stirs and stirs, trying to get the cocoa to dissolve, but it never really does. Finally I tell him it doesn't matter—I can drink it as it is. Which I regret as soon as I take my first sip.

After summer vacation, I start fifth grade, and Holst begins teaching at my school. I have him for geography. It's strange seeing him at school. I don't know how to address him, so I avoid him as much as possible. No one in class knows that I go over to Holst's—we haven't talked about how to discuss it—so we both act like everything's normal. In class I answer just like everyone else, and at home we don't discuss what we're learning in class. The other students are afraid of him: he gives a lot of homework, and his voice is stern if you come to class unprepared.

Another exciting thing happens after summer vacation: Bodil joins our class. Bodil moved to Birket with her mother, who's a housekeeper for the people who own the orchard. Bodil's mother and father are divorced, and Bodil's father still lives on a farm outside of Sakskøbing. Bodil is exciting. She has short, wild red hair, big blue eyes, and is at least a head taller than me. She's thirteen, over a year older than me, so she's already started her period. Bodil sits next to me—and from the very first day, we spend recess together. I finally have a friend.

Bodil has her own really nice room. Her mother's whole house is nicely decorated. We're not allowed to do a lot of things in that house, because we can't do anything that might create dust. We can't sit in the living room, we're not allowed to dance, we can't run, and we aren't allowed to have pillow fights. It's the first time I've been made aware of what causes dust. Not that I do anything like that very often at Holst's, but it can get pretty crazy when I'm playing with Troll.

At Bodil's, however, we're not allowed to run through the living room, so we just walk quickly, giggling loudly the whole time. If Bodil's mother yells at us for creating dust by walking too quickly, Bodil asks her if she wants us to crawl through the living room. Bodil's pretty fresh to her mother in a way that makes me double over with laughter. She's so funny.

Bodil and I soon discover that the harbor at Kragenæs is the place to be. I've never biked down there by myself. Every summer, they have a harbor festival, and there are a lot of tourists all summer long. What's most exciting are the boys who hang out by the harbor kiosk every night. They're crazy about Bodil, although they don't even look at me. We cycle down to the harbor every evening. I usually keep one hand on Bodil's arm so she can pull me along; she's strong and rides fast, whereas I have to struggle to catch my breath. Sometimes she takes her feet off the pedals until I catch up. Then she'll give me a good shove in the back, so I'll pick up some speed, and we laugh and cheer. Bodil is so funny.

Before long we become part of the group that hangs out at the harbor. We mostly talk to three guys: Tom, his big brother, and Kykli. Kykli, who's older than the others, is thin and has long, greasy hair, round metal glasses, and a thin, patchy beard. He has a car too. Almost every night the five of us drive around with Kykli at the wheel, if we're not standing down by the kiosk, drinking beer and smoking cigarettes. Red Looks. Bodil and I only buy cigarettes and Dandy chewing gum. Our new friends buy the beer. It's the first time I've ever drunk beer. It doesn't taste good, but the chewing gum counteracts it somewhat. I've never smoked cigarettes before either, but Bodil shows me how to smoke without sucking on the filter and how to inhale. Not that I haven't had offers to smoke before. All three of my brothers smoke, and they've tried to entice me several times, but with Bodil and the guys at the harbor, it just feels "right" and far more exciting.

I'm busy every day. I have my schoolwork, and Bodil and I often do our homework together. When we're at the harbor, we tell Bodil's mother she's sleeping over with me. But it can get pretty late before we actually go to bed at my house, so I'm tired in the morning. Still, we go to school every day, even if we're not always at our best.

Whenever we sleep at Bodil's, we go to bed much earlier. We lie there and talk. One night I tell her I don't like sleeping with the lights off and that I'd like her to look for ghosts or anything else that might be hiding under the bed and in the closet—and that she needs to do it three times and in a certain order. She laughs so hard she cries, but she does as I ask. Oddly enough, I laugh, too, while I tell her I don't know why I'm like this, but it helps me sleep. She says she understands. I love sleeping with Bodil; sometimes we hold hands while we sleep.

I don't tell Bodil that I'm seeing Holst and Ragna. I go there less often now, but enough that it still feels natural. They never ask what Bodil and I are doing. They don't even seem surprised that I'm not coming over as much.

I don't want Bodil in the house when Jan's there. She can't meet Jan. I still sleep in the double bed, which Bodil doesn't know either. Jan and Mom are still having wild sex at night when they go to bed, and more and more frequently Jan pulls off my comforter in the dark and crawls down between my legs first. Once he reaches a certain point, he moves over to Mom, and they have sex while I turn my back to them. One night, when Mom has to go pee in the middle of everything, Jan stands up and tells me to sit on the edge of the bed. He grabs his penis, which is stiff, and moves it around my privates without sticking it in, all the while staring at me. I look away.

"Do you like that?" he asks, breathing heavily.

I don't respond. He keeps doing it while getting closer to my hole, so that his penis almost goes in. It doesn't hurt.

"Jytte!" he yells, calling for my mother. "Come and look at this."

Mom comes back in and looks terrified. "Be careful—if you do that it could be evidence."

He pulls back quickly, and I say I have to pee. When I come back, Mom and Jan are yelling at each other in the living room. Mom says: "I'm going to fucking turn you in to the police, you pervert!"

Jan roars with laughter. "They can't prove anything. And they sure as hell won't listen to you. Anyway, you've been part of it too."

In February of 1980, I turn twelve, so Bodil and I decide to have a party. We take the bus to the Aldi in Maribo and buy a case of beer and a few bags of chips, which we struggle to carry back to the bus. Bodil is strong, but I'm not—and we almost give up because the handle on the case is cutting into my hand. We do make it, although barely, and laughing and out of breath, we climb onto the bus. Once home, we put the case of beer in the kitchen. Bodil's at my house when Mom comes home that night. She goes right into the kitchen, and I suddenly wonder how she's going to react to our buying a case of beer. She comes into the living room and asks whose beer it is.

"Bodil's and mine. They're for my birthday," I say.

"Okay," says Mom. "Can I take a few?"

"Yes," we say in unison.

Tom, Tom's older brother, and Kykli come to the party. We told them we're celebrating my twelfth birthday, so they've brought beer too. It's a little strange to play host. We put music on the stereo, put chips in bowls, and light some candles. Bodil and I start dancing while the three guys watch. Bodil is an unbelievable dancer, and we've developed our own jitterbug, in which Bodil mostly twirls me around. We drink beer, and before long we're dizzy and light-headed. Tom and his big brother dance with us too, and we all laugh and sing. At some point, we decide we should take a ride in Kykli's car. We drive fast, but Kykli is a good driver, so I'm not afraid. We drive back to my place, so we can drink and dance some more. Suddenly I get really tired; I can barely stand up, and I stagger over to the sofa to lie down. Kykli gets up off the chair where he's been sitting and watching the whole time we've been dancing. He walks over, carefully lifts me up in his arms, and carries me to Mom's bed. He pulls off my clothes, wraps the comforter around me, and gives me a kiss on the cheek. He leaves, and I fall asleep drunk, tired, and comfy.

The next thing I hear about Kykli is that he shot himself in the mouth with a shotgun.

The days pass. I divide them up as best I can between Bodil, Holst, school, and my mother. I try to keep the four parts of my life separate, and I don't tell anyone what I'm doing. Bodil is the one who knows the most about my life.

For a while, Mom starts coming home with different men. I barely pay any attention. Jan shows up sometimes, and that usually ends in yelling and fighting. Mom is tired of him, but I don't think she can get him to stay away.

One day Mom has a new man with her and she seems really different. She's elated. His name is Richard—and I get it. He looks like that Eurovision singer, Bjørn Tidmand. He's small, and he has broad shoulders and blue eyes. Mom is in love. Jan doesn't show up anymore, probably because of Richard. He's the type who makes you feel a little scared, but in a good way. You try a little harder when he's around. He never says anything, and when he finally does, you jump to please him. I know he has a daughter about my age and a small son.

Richard is a farmhand who lives in a small house that belongs to the farm where he works. It's a nice house with wall-to-wall carpeting and a ton of medals for billiards and marksmanship on the bookshelves. In one corner, between the shelves and the wall, he keeps a number of weapons that he uses when he's hunting, shooting clay pigeons, or in the national guard. He also has a shotgun he lets me borrow. I stand in his garden and shoot at different targets. He shows me how to load and take aim, and he warns me that if I ever shoot at anything other than the target, he won't answer for the consequences. I only shoot at the target, and I'm already a pretty good shot.

Mom isn't home as much. Richard lives even farther away than Jan, so if Mom calls at all, it's usually to ask if I can sleep at Holst's or at Bodil's. Sometimes I'm home alone; I stand at the window staring at the passing headlights to see if it might be Richard's car. I can tell his headlights from a distance. They're yellower than most headlights—like yellow teeth.

Mom drinks at least as much with Richard as she did with Jan. Still, I get the feeling that it's less of a problem for Mom and Richard. That feeling only lasts until the day I'm with Mom and Richard at a bar called Lido in Nakskov. Lido is Richard's hangout; he goes to that bar every day, and wherever he goes, he's king. That's what he says—and I believe him. You can see the respect people show him when he enters a room.

It's one of the first really sunny summer days. Mom has on a top and a pair of tight short-shorts. She loves the sun and goes sunbathing the first moment it peeks through the clouds. She always gets dark brown in record time. Mom has been lying in Richard's garden all afternoon this Saturday while I've been practicing with the shotgun. You can see that she's gotten sun. She looks great with her brown skin and shiny white dentures. Mom and Richard make a pretty nice-looking couple. Mom's in a good mood, so she puts some coins in the jukebox and dances to the music. I dance along and we're having fun. Mom is drinking hard, though, and I can tell that she enjoys having other men look at her. Richard, who has been lost in playing craps, suddenly looks up at Mom. His gaze darkens, and he says: "Tone it down a little, Jytte." Everyone in the bar seems to freeze.

Mom stares at him and sneers. "That coming from you, you little sissy!" I count and count and hope it helps.

It doesn't. Richard stands up, walks quickly over to Mom, and slaps her. There are at least ten other people in the place, and no one says or does anything. The music has stopped now. Mom grabs her head, looks at him, and yells as loudly as she can in his face: "Can't you hit any harder than that, you little sissy?"

Richard grabs one of the straps of her top—and it falls down to her stomach. Mom's not wearing a bra, so she's suddenly standing there with her breasts exposed. He grabs one of her breasts and starts twisting it around until she screams and falls to her knees. Then he lifts her up by the arm, hard, and shoves her out the door, saying: "Hit the road—you and your kid." I run after Mom and help her put her top back on. She cries and wants to go back in, but I calm her down and call for a taxi to drive us home. Mom goes right to bed. I really feel bad for her. She was just in a good mood and wanted to dance. I know how much she likes Richard—I can't understand why he would embarrass her that way. And why didn't anybody in the bar stop him?

The next day, Richard shows up. Mom flutters around him and is happy. I stay in my room for most of the day, except when I go out for my usual walk, to smoke a cigarette and count. Nothing happens, though, and the whole episode at Lido seems like something I dreamed.

One day Mom informs me that she and Richard aren't seeing each other anymore. Now she's seeing someone named Henning. Shortly thereafter, there's another, and then one day Richard is back again. I don't care. As long as I don't have to deal with her and her men and can spend my time at Holst's or with Bodil.

Right before summer vacation, Holst pulls me aside in the school hall-way. It's recess, so I'm surprised he wants to talk. He leads me over to a window and hands me a small piece of paper with a telephone number on it; he tells me it's the number for the township—that I can always call if I'm having a hard time at home. I don't say anything to Bodil. After school, I ride straight home and make the call, but as I dial the number, I start having doubts. I'm afraid of hurting Mom, yet I'd really like to be living like my brothers, who had smelled so nice when they came home from the orphanage on the weekends. Also, I start to think it might be a relief for Mom if I'm gone. A caseworker at the township answers the phone, and I explain that I got the number from Holst. I tell her that things aren't good at home, and the woman says that some-one at the orphanage in Nakskov will come and get me in a few hours. I pack a bag and put my schoolbag next to it while I wait.

Suddenly Mom comes home with Richard, who has driven her here. The township must have called her. She races into the living room and starts yelling at me. I'm standing in my usual spot by the window, watching for the van from the orphanage. Actually, I don't think Mom has ever screamed at me before. I yell back at her, as loudly as I can, that I don't want to be here anymore—that she's evil. She cries even more. I quickly regret what I said; she's definitely not evil.

Two hours later, I'm on my way to the orphanage, the two bags by my feet.

1980—81

As we drive down the wide road leading to the orphanage, I recognize everything from the last time, and from the times when I've visited my brothers. They don't live here anymore. Tonny is with Dad in Køge, René's in a foster home in Karise, and Michael's at a youth hostel in Copenhagen (when he hasn't run off somewhere).

I'll be living in Family Group, where there's room for about thirteen children. I'm wondering why I'm not back in the section I lived in last time—the one down by the playground. They tell me that I'll be in Family Group, where they try to create a family atmosphere, because children stay there for a long time.

I walk behind an adult in a tiled hallway that runs the length of the house. I try not to step on any lines, and I count every tile. Screams suddenly shake me out of my counting. To my right, just before the entrance to Family Group, there's a large window, and through it I can see at least twenty parakeets flying around inside a room. It's amazing! These birds actually have their own room at the orphanage. At least ten birdhouses are hanging on the back wall, and there are perches, trees, and swings all over the place. I also notice that two of the parakeets are blue, whereas all the others are green and yellow. The blue parakeets are the most beautiful.

I'm lost in my own thoughts when the adult suddenly calls to me. "Come on, Lisbeth, now you'll meet the children and adults you'll be with from now on."

Family Group is to the left, just inside the main entrance. The first thing I notice is how clean it smells—there isn't a speck of dust or a spot of dirt anywhere. I like that. The adult follows me in, and two other grown-ups immediately walk over. They both say "Hi," and offer me their hands.

They introduce themselves as Mette and Jørgen. Jørgen says he's going to be my primary social worker: he's the one I can come to if I have any problems or if I need help with school or my mother. Naturally, the other social workers will help me too, but he deals with the bigger issues.

The first thing Jørgen does is show me my new room. "You can put your bags in there," he says. We walk down a hallway that seems to split in the middle. Family Group consists of two hallways that meet on a diagonal. On my way down to my room, I pass a small, cozy kitchen, and right where the hallway splits there's an entrance to a living room with two long dining tables and a group of sofas. The room also has a patio facing a large soccer field surrounded by tall bushes. Just beyond the split there's a common entrance with a small lobby. There are two small rooms here, and mine is to the left. A boy named Fini, who has golden hair and is a little younger than me, lives to the right.

Jørgen tells me I'll get a larger room once someone moves, but newbies usually get one of these two rooms. I'm happy enough with this room. The walls are papered with burlap, and there's a platform bed with a mattress covered in orange corduroy, a small desk, a blue backless desk chair, and a closet. At the end of the room a window takes up the whole wall, so I can see the entire soccer field. No one is playing now, but I think it will be nice to sit and look out when kids are playing.

Jørgen asks if I'd like to go with him to the living room for choco-late cake, juice, and coffee, and to meet the other children. Jørgen and

Mette walk around calling for the children who are home, and they run into the room. We all sit down by the light-colored wood table while we enjoy the juice and cake. Jørgen tells the others my name, and introduces them to me. Thank God I don't have to say anything. I glance around at the other kids while we eat.

Two of the boys are named Kim. Kim Oskar—who's about my age—gives me a big smile. The other Kim is seventeen; he gives me an angry look when he's introduced. I'll be avoiding him. Then there's Darius, who speaks Danish with a Polish accent. Darius is a few years older than me and seems friendly. There are also two boys named Michael. One's a day student who has his own instructional support teacher; he behaves just like my aunt in Copenhagen—I think they have the same problems. The other Michael is cross-eyed. His lips are dark red and always wet. When he looks at something, he turns his head like a parrot and stares with one eye. He doesn't really look at me when we're introduced. He just sits there reading a train schedule. There's Robin, who's about my age; he loves to play chess and wants to teach me. And then there's Stig, who's sixteen, covered with pimples, and who gives me a strange, empty stare. There aren't any girls, but that's not a problem. I'm used to boys.

I notice that four of the boys start smoking after we've eaten cake, so the cigarettes and ashtrays come out. Even though I smoke too, I haven't told the social workers, so I don't join them. After cake, Jørgen takes me down to the caseworkers' office; while writing in a file, he tells me a little about the daily routines in Family Group. Everyone is assigned to small groups that take turns helping with dinner. Most of the groups have two children and one adult—but we're an uneven number of children right now, so I'll be alone in one group with a social worker.

"Why?" I ask.

"Because you're the only girl," says Jørgen, "so it makes sense that you're in a group by yourself with your own social worker."

"I think that's unfair," I say.

He doesn't respond. Instead, he tells me that we have to wash our own clothes, with some help from a short, fat woman named Birger. We get an allowance every Friday, but if we don't do our chores, it's taken out of our allowance. Finally he asks me if I need anything, if there's anything I can't tolerate, and if I smoke. I say no to all of it while hiding my hands so he can't see my warts.

I sneak a glance at Jørgen. He's older than my mother yet doesn't seem old. His hair is jet-black, he has blue eyes, and his teeth are white as a sheet. When he smiles, you're almost blinded by his white teeth and a little bit of gold on one of his front teeth. He smiles a lot. I'm happy he's my caseworker.

He gives me permission to walk around a little on my own. I go over to the living room where Big Kim and Stig are each lying on a sofa, smoking and talking while listening to heavy metal. There aren't any social workers in there. I want to check out the games I can see in the bookcase. As soon as I step into the room, Kim turns around, gets up quickly, grabs a book from a shelf, and hurls it at me, yelling at me to get the fuck out. He says this room belongs to him and Stig. Although the book doesn't hit me, I'm still in shock. Stig, who's lying on the other sofa, just stares at me. I hurry back to my room with my heart pounding and my hands shaking.

I stay in my room, where I unpack my clothes and put them in the closet. I sit down at my desk and try to draw but soon become bored. I decide to sneak out of the room again to go look at the room with the birds. The glass door leading to the birds is locked; I'd like to try standing in the middle of a flock of birds whirling around me.

The door to Family Group suddenly opens and, frightened, I turn around. I don't want to run into Big Kim out here where there aren't any other people, but it's just Kim Oskar. He walks over, stands next to me, and stares at the birds.

He points at the birdhouses. "There are eggs in most of them."

"How do you know that?" I ask.

"Because we take turns cleaning the aviary, and when it's my turn, I check on the eggs," he replies.

I decide to ask Jørgen if I can clean up in there too. Kim takes out a pack of cigarettes and offers me one. I accept and Kim lights it for me.

"Just tell me if you run out of smokes," he says.

I like him.

After dinner, it's time to take a bath and unpack my bag. I have all my books from the old school. I left so fast to come to the orphanage that I never got to return them. I take them out and place them in a pile on my desk; then I clean out my red schoolbag so all that's left are a pencil case and a couple of notebooks. Jørgen comes to tell me he'll be off soon but another social worker is coming on duty. Her name is Kirsten. He says she'll be awake all night, so I mustn't be afraid—if I need anything, I can just walk down to the office.

While I'm taking off my clothes, I wonder if I'm ever going to see the Holsts again. I don't even know if they know I've moved. I also wonder if my mother is still crying and how I'm going to tell Bodil that I won't be in school at Birket anymore. I'm going to miss her and Holst. I want to talk to Jørgen about that tomorrow.

I think about how I should sleep—with my door open or shut? I decide to keep the door slightly ajar and then check three times for ghosts behind the curtains, in the closet, and under the bed. Afterward, I crawl beneath the comforter but leave the light on. Jørgen knocks softly on the door and sits on the edge of my bed. He looks at me for a while and asks if I'm okay.

"Yes," I say, "but I'm worried Holst doesn't know I've left home."

"Holst knows," he says. "We've spoken to him, and Holst and his wife will be coming to visit you soon."

I'm happy to hear that. Jørgen strokes my hair, tucks the comforter around me, and slips out, leaving the door slightly ajar.

I must have fallen asleep. Suddenly I wake up with a start. Someone is in my room. It's Stig, sitting in his underpants at my desk and staring at me. I look over at the door and see that it's completely closed now. He says I mustn't be afraid. I just have to lie still and it will go fast. I'm terrified. He pulls down my comforter and my underpants and then pulls down his own. He tries to stick a finger in me, but I say "ouch!" so loudly that he jumps. He lies between my legs and starts licking me while he masturbates. He ejaculates immediately, almost without a sound, and then he stands up, pulls up his underpants, and dries off his finger on my comforter. He looks down at me and says: "Fuck, you taste like shit. And keep your mouth shut about it." Then he leaves, closing the door behind him.

I get up and shove my desk chair against the door; that way I'll wake up if anyone tries to open it. Tomorrow I'll have to find a real chair with a back that I can put underneath the door handle when I'm sleeping.

The next morning I go to my new school, Stormarksskolen, for the first time. A social worker named Lotte is on duty in the mornings. She's young and has short, dark hair and a very beautiful face with strong features. She's a sharp dresser in tight black pants and a formfitting, long-sleeved white sweater. Lotte tells me how to get breakfast, which is already laid out on a table in the living room, and how to prepare a lunch box. While we're eating, she says that she'll be walking with me to school today. On the way to school—which is only five hundred yards from the orphanage—she points at a side street and says that she lives there. Her husband is working on a drilling site abroad, and she rides a motorcycle. Lotte is so cool.

Lotte walks me all the way to class, where we say hello to my new homeroom teacher, Grethe. The other children are already in their seats. Grethe points to a spot that's still empty in the middle of the room and says: "You can sit next to Heidi—she's promised to show you around school today." I look down at Heidi. She's a freckled, round-cheeked girl with long, dark, and wildly curly hair. Heidi smiles widely and pats the chair next to her. At recess I walk around with Heidi and a few other girls, and during classes I scrutinize the other students. We're eight girls and six boys. Everyone seems pretty peaceful, except Steen and Allan, who cause trouble and get yelled at in all of our classes. I decide to avoid them. It's pretty clear that they target their victims—and I don't want to become one of them.

After school I walk home. Heidi asked if I want to get together tomorrow after school, which really made me happy. As I walk into my section of the building, I can hear my mother's voice coming from inside the living room. "He's a psychopath and I wanted to take control of my own life, so I left him," she's saying. I walk into the room and say hello. "Hi there, Mouse," Mom exclaims. I hate when she calls me Mouse. "I just stopped by to see how you're doing."

She turns around again and continues talking to Lotte about Richard. I hitch up my schoolbag and go into my room. A little while later, Lotte comes in and asks how it went at school.

"Good," I say. "I'm already going home with a girl named Heidi tomorrow."

"Fantastic," says Lotte. "I know Heidi well. We live on the same street. Stop in if you want to. Heidi knows where it is."

Lotte isn't just cool and beautiful—she's really sweet too. She asks if I'd like to come into the living room and get a piece of French bread and talk to my mother. I sit and listen while my mother goes on and on about Richard. I try to find out if she's angry that I called the township yesterday. After some time she looks at me and says she needs to get going. Then she empties her coffee cup, stubs out her smoke, and puts on her jacket.

"You take care, Mouse. I'll stop by again tomorrow."

She tousles my hair and scurries out the door. I never even get to say I'm going over to Heidi's tomorrow. I don't even get to show her my room.

Days pass at both the orphanage and my new school. Stig hasn't touched me again, and I avoid the room with him and Big Kim. My classmates have accepted me—except for Steen and Allan, whom I ignore. I can keep up with my lessons, and I especially love Danish. I really like my homeroom and Danish teacher, Grethe, who always says I'm quite good at Danish. I spell well, my writing is neat, and I have a good handle on the grammar. My goal is to be the best in my class, so homework comes before everything else—even spending time with Heidi. Math is hard, though; it makes no sense to me. In the other subjects, I can grasp things before I even do the assignments—but math is a mystery. I'm in sixth grade and I'm still counting on my fingers.

Grethe attends a meeting at the orphanage with Jørgen, a psychologist, the principal (Britta), and me. Grethe says that I'm functioning really well in my class and that I'm doing well academically too. They also say that I'm doing well at the orphanage, although now and then I get angry for no reason. They add that surely it's because I'm entering puberty, but maybe I should think about trying to be less angry. I tell them that I'm not angry when I have to do my chores, which they confirm, but that I get angry when they suddenly change plans, or interfere in my life, or are unfair. For example, when the boys get more help doing the laundry than I do—or how there are more of them to help make food than when it's my turn to do it. I especially hate any changes in plans.

I know I'm stubborn—Mom's always telling me that—and I hate change. Like when we've arranged a trip to Knuthenborg Safari Park and it's canceled because of changes in staffing, or when someone quits or gets sick at school and we have substitutes. Something as simple as changes in mealtimes without telling me beforehand can make me furious. I don't know why, but that's how I am. And I hate to be told what to do. I know I have chores to do—but aside from that, the adults need to stay out of my business.

One time I got some money to buy shoes, and I came home with a pair of high-heeled sandals in a beautiful blue color. Mette walked into my room and asked if she could see my new shoes. When she saw them, she told me to go back into town and exchange them: they looked cheap and I was too young for high heels. I took the box with the shoes in it and threw it across the room, and then I told her to get the hell out. I get so angry that my blood boils—and when I get like that, I tend to react in one of two ways: throw things around or shut down completely.

At the meeting, we also discuss Mom coming here every day. At first I feel obligated to talk to her, but after a few weeks of her being here whenever I come home from school, I just give her a quick hello. She's usually sitting in the living room drinking coffee, smoking, and talking to whatever social worker happens to be sitting there listening. I just go right to my room, if I don't go into Darius's to play cards with him and Kim Oskar, or to listen to Darius's stereo. The good thing about Mom coming all the time is that she usually gives me money and cigarettes. Otherwise I'm tired of hearing her voice every day. She's always talking about Richard, who's either fantastic or a psychopath, depending on her mood.

Jørgen promises to set some rules for how often Mom can come. Soon she's rarely coming—but I see her when I go home every other weekend to Richard's house.

At first Mom says that I can come home as soon as Richard converts the loft in his house into a room for me. I tell Jørgen that I really don't want to move back home with them. He says he totally understands.

A short time later, I have a meeting with a clinical psychologist who wants to test my personality and intelligence. The psychologist, whose name is Lars, is a really nice man. We talk for a while and he asks me to solve some tasks. It's a lot of fun. He also asks how it's going with my mother. I tell him: "It's like there's a wall between my mother and me that I can't break through. We just don't see eye to eye." The meeting is just between Lars and me. He asks where I'd like to go in the future. I tell him I want to go into foster care; that's my greatest wish.

I don't recall much about my time with Grethe and her husband, Otto, but I always get a warm feeling whenever I think of them. The same with the Holsts. René is living with a foster family, and I hear he's doing well. Lars says that it makes sense—and that he'll tell the orphanage that's what I want to do.

After our meeting, I actually feel a little taller. The rest of the day I'm elated. I even talk with Michael about his obsession with train schedules—something I rarely do because once he gets started it's hard to break away.

A little while later, Jørgen tells me that they've arranged it so that Mom can't take me home unless it's what I want. Also, they're going to talk to Mom about a foster family.

One Saturday, Bodil comes to visit. We haven't seen each other for a long time, but the visit is weird. It feels like we've both changed. We can't seem to relax around each other, and I think she seems more grown up. We take a walk through Nakskov and window-shop a little. It's a Saturday afternoon, so everything's closed except Frellsen Chocolate, where we buy some candy. Then I walk her to the bus stop. Neither of us suggests getting together again.

Instead of going home, I walk over to Lido, where I find Mom and Richard. I get a soda and some smokes from Mom. All afternoon, I sit and watch Mom play pool while Richard shoots craps. We get French fries too, and I play the one-armed bandit. Richard knows the owners, so I get all the tokens I want, as long as I return them if I win.

Suddenly I realize that it's long past suppertime at the orphanage; I say goodbye to Mom and Richard and hurry back. When I get there, Kirsten, another one of the social workers, is waiting—and she's angry that I wasn't home for dinner. I stare at her while she stands there yelling at me, wondering if I should explode or just ignore her. I choose the latter. I go to my room to get my overcoat and then head back to Mom and Richard at the bar. They don't say anything, and I go back home with them. The next day I return to the orphanage, where I learn that Jørgen wants to have a meeting with me to discuss my behavior. Also, I have to stay home for the rest of that Sunday. I don't even respond. I just head straight for Darius's room, where Kim Oskar is, and we stay there all day, smoking and listening to music.

As Christmas approaches, I ask if I can spend the holiday with Dad, whom I haven't seen in a long time. Jørgen asks Mom if I can spend Christmas with Dad, but Mom says no way. I have to spend the holidays with Richard and her. She wants to play house with Richard.

Mom makes roast pork. She bustles around Richard constantly and chatters away incessantly, while Richard says nothing. He's even less approachable than usual. Mom and I bought gifts a few days before Christmas, and they're sitting in one corner of the living room. There's no Christmas tree, because Christmas means nothing to Richard. After dinner, he sits down and stares at the TV until he closes his eyes and falls asleep. I ask when we're opening gifts. "When Richard wakes up," replies Mom.

A little while later, he comes to, and Mom asks him to go out to the garage and get my gift. He gets up like a sleepwalker and soon comes back in struggling with something that looks like a wrapped mattress. I rip off the paper. It's a brand-new bike! My first. I give Mom a big hug, but she says Richard paid for most of it, so he's the one who deserves the hug. He doesn't seem like a hugger, so I just say thanks. He grunts back, all the while staring at the TV he sat back down in front of as soon as I started unwrapping my gift.

Now it's time for Mom to open her gifts. I bought her a top and three pairs of G-string panties. She unwraps them and says, "Oh, how nice," all the while winking at me. Richard mustn't find out that she's the one who chose them. Now she unwraps her gift from Richard. She bought it for herself, since Richard doesn't buy gifts. It's a light-colored leather wallet.

"Ohhhh!" she exclaims, and then she walks over and gives Richard a kiss.

"Get lost!" he hisses, shoving her away.

I can tell he's about to vomit over the whole charade. Now it's time for Richard's gifts. Mom bought him a number of things—I got him an ashtray. I take my gift and hand it to him, but he just keeps staring at the screen as he says: "I *told* you that I don't celebrate Christmas and I don't want any gifts." I put the package back on his pile of gifts. When I wake up the next morning, the packages are all gone. Mom says that he opened them while we were sleeping.

Richard has guests over every night during the holidays. The first night I wake up because I have to pee. As I walk downstairs, I see a lot of people in the house. Some are standing around in the kitchen and talking, while others are sitting around the dining room table. They're playing cards, and the table is covered with dirty ashtrays, coffee cups, and beer bottles. There are thick wads of money next to several of the players. I've never seen so much money before. Out in the kitchen, Mom is making a huge platter of sandwiches.

"What are you doing here?" she asks.

"I have to pee," I say, slipping into the toilet at the back of the kitchen.

After I'm done, I go back into the living room and watch the people. They play cards every night of the holiday, and every night I sneak out to watch them. During the day, Richard teaches me how to play five hundred, thirty-one, eleven-and-a-half, and casino.

Several times during the holidays, Mom mentions that I'll be moving home soon, but I don't say anything. Finally she asks: "Don't you want to?"

"Of course," I reply, but I mean no. I just don't want to hurt her. She's trying to play house with Richard—it's much better than when she was married to Jan, but they still fight, argue, and drink too much.

By the time I go back to the orphanage, I'm tired and depressed. Night and day have been turned upside down. A few days later, Mom comes to visit and tells the adults that I want to move back home. Jørgen, who's working that day, asks me if it's true. "Yes," I say while looking at Mom. I really wish he had asked me when she wasn't there. He suggests that I pack a few things and take an extra-long vacation at home and think about it before we make a final decision. I go to my room to pack.

Mom and Richard are at the bar almost every day, and I'm usually with them. I go there straight from school and take my schoolbag with me. I do my homework at the bar, and we eat there too. Thanks to Richard's card games, Mom and he have a lot of money at this point—that's why we're able to eat out most days.

One night at home, they're both drunk and start arguing about something. Suddenly Richard jumps up and smacks Mom. She tumbles onto the television, which falls over. The picture of Richard and his ex-wife and their daughter crashes to the ground. Richard turns bright red. He knocks Mom around the room, so that she's falling over all the furniture. "I'll fucking kill you!" he screams, struggling to stay on his feet between punches. "I don't care if I have to lose ten years of my life to get rid of you."

I'm sure he's going to kill her—and if he does, he'll kill me too. I lock myself in the bathroom. My hands are shaking so much I have trouble turning the key. I can still hear her tumbling all around the living room. Suddenly everything's quiet. *She must be dead,* I think, and have no idea what I should do. I listen at the door but can't hear anything.

Slowly, I unlock the door and slip out into the kitchen. Then they start up again in the bedroom. I hear Mom groan. As I reach the bedroom door, I see her head strike a sharp corner on the headboard. A thin stream of blood springs like a fountain from between her fingers, staining the bright bedsheets. Silently, she lies down on the bed with one hand on her head.

Richard, pale as a ghost, sits down on a chair. Paralyzed, I stand there staring at the grotesque scene; then I come to and yell at him to get some towels. I hold a few of them against Mom's head and scream at him to call an ambulance. A moment later the front door slams and his car starts. I sit with my hands pressed against Mom's head in the bedroom until I hear the ambulance. My whole body is shaking and my teeth are chattering.

I accompany her to the emergency room, where she gets stitches. At the hospital, they say she's free to go home. As soon as we're out of the emergency room, Mom wants to see Richard at the Axe, so I go with her. Richard is standing at the bar. As we walk in, Mom says "Hi" loudly, smiling at everyone.

Richard turns around. "Something to drink?"

I don't want anything. I storm out of there. I'm furious with both of them. I pack my things and ride my bike back to the orphanage. Once there, I tell them that I don't want to live with my mother and that she pressured me to say I did. I don't say anything about the visit to the emergency room.

Heidi and I continue to hang out after school and even take a self-defense class taught by her father at the gym. I learn to do a dive roll, the nun's prayer, and a judo throwing technique. It's a lot of fun.

One night I find a bag in the locker room while we're on a break. Heidi and I are the only ones in the room. Inside the bag are a wallet, a pack of cigarettes, and a set of car keys. I take the cigarettes and put the money from the wallet in my own bag. Heidi says that's really stupid—but I say that the woman shouldn't leave things lying around like an invitation. I walk back over to the bag, grab the car keys, and toss them as far as I can out the window and into the dark.

"Why did you do that?" asks Heidi.

"I don't know," I reply, laughing. "Let's go back to the others."

A little while later, the woman comes in with two men from the gym. They call for Heidi and me, and her father comes with us. Out in the hallway, they ask if we're the ones who stole things from the woman's purse. Heidi cries and says yes. I don't say anything. As they stand there yelling at us, my mind starts to wander. I don't come back to until they've repeatedly asked me where the car keys are. They shove us out into the dark to search for the keys, which we can't find.

The men from the gym tell us we're banned from using the gym for six months. I don't care—but I'm sad that Heidi isn't allowed to see me anymore.

After that incident, I spend a lot of weekends with the Holsts. In the evenings we watch TV together, and I always go to bed early. I feel tired and lazy around them—in the best possible way. I sleep more and better at the Holsts' than in the orphanage or at home with Mom and Richard.

I take the same walks as when I lived in Torrig, which gives me time to smoke two cigarettes. I haven't told Holst that I smoke. While I walk, I think about what I want to do with my future. I want an education—maybe to become an aircraft mechanic. I've read that you have to use your hands and be smart to do that job. That sounds perfect for me, so I decide to take metal shop.

In eighth grade, I start metal shop classes. Most of the girls choose needlework or typing. My teachers, classmates, and the social workers all think it's crazy, but I don't care.

My metal shop teacher thinks it's funny that I make totally different things than the boys do. I make jewelry and ashtrays, along with a really nice birdhouse that I bend and polish so it has no sharp edges—all in copper.

I'm responsible for the aviary at the orphanage now. It happened when I told Jørgen that I wanted to clean up in there so I'd get to be with the birds. After the first cleaning, when I removed bird droppings that had been sitting there for years, Jørgen suggested I take the job permanently. He could see how happy I was to be around the birds. I said yes—on one condition: that I get the birds. He asked what I meant by "get the birds." I told him I didn't want to take the birds with me—I just wanted to be the one in the orphanage who made decisions about them. He agreed to that.

The day I finish the birdhouse, Jan—my constant tormentor in metal shop—laughs loudly and says that any bird trying to fly in there will have its head chopped off by the sharp metal edge running around the hole. I ignore him until he comes over to my side of the workbench, knocks the birdhouse to the floor, and then kicks it under the table. I don't think he realizes that I take self-defense classes. Anyway, he looks somewhat surprised when I put a police hold on him. Holding one of his arms behind his back, I guide him slowly along the floor while I ask him to use his other arm to pick up the birdhouse—which he does while the other boys stand around laughing.

Unfortunately, Steen and Allan see what I've done to Jan. I have no idea why they think they have to seek vengeance for him, but a few days later while we're riding our bikes to the school dentist—without any adults—they waylay me just before we reach the dentist's office. "You think you're so smart, Lisbeth," says Allan, "but you're nothing but a fucking orphan who thinks she's big shit." Steen grabs my arms from behind and holds me while Allan punches my stomach several times. Holding my stomach, I fall down as they run off. Nobody saw what happened. Once I've recovered, I bike home.

Once again, Jørgen holds a meeting with my caseworker from the township, the social workers, and my homeroom teacher, Grethe. All of them say it's going poorly. Grethe heard about the episode in metal shop. I tell them that they obviously don't understand my situation—what else can you expect from a bunch of hillbillies who've become social workers because they're too stupid to do anything else. I ask them how it's going with finding me a foster family. Jørgen replies that my mother doesn't want me in a foster family. She's afraid she'll lose all connection to me, yet I can't come home, either, because of the way I've been acting out because of all my issues.

"My only 'issue' is this orphanage that doesn't understand it needs to leave me alone," I respond, purposely emphasizing the word "issue."

Ridiculous nonsense. Ridiculous people. Grethe suddenly suggests that I could move home with her. I'm shocked. Does she really want me—with all my issues? Jørgen says we'll have to talk about that at another meeting, and we pack up.

A few days later, Grethe asks if I want to go home with her after school. She has to pick up something and then she has to go back to Nakskov. Grethe's house is in a small village. A modern yellow suburban house, it reminds me a little of our home in Køge, where we lived with Jan. Only bigger.

Grethe lives alone with her four-year-old daughter, Louise. While Grethe is gathering what she needs, I walk around the house and imagine what it would be like to live there. The house is clean and bright—and it smells nice too. As Grethe drops me off at the orphanage, she tells me that she's going to a meeting there tomorrow about the possibility of bringing me home with her. I can barely sleep that night.

The next day after school, Grethe and I walk together back to the orphanage. We go into the conference room and say goodbye. The conference room is next to the aviary, so I spend the wait cleaning up after the birds.

A little while later, Grethe and Jørgen come back out, and I ask how it went. Jørgen says that Grethe can't take me into her care because she lives alone with her daughter. He says Grethe is disappointed. I stare at Jørgen for a long time, and then I slam the glass door and walk out.

One day we get a new student in class. Jette. She has long, dark hair and strong features, just like Lotte at the orphanage. Jette will be sitting in the empty seat next to me. I told Grethe I'd show Jette around during recess. When the bell rings, Jette asks where you can smoke. I laugh and say we're not allowed—but I know a place behind the school where we won't be bothered. Jette and I talk about cigarettes, stupid parents, and boys. Jette has already had a boyfriend and slept with him. I tell her I haven't tried it yet. I could never discuss what's already happened—and anyway that wasn't with any boyfriend.

After school, I walk back home with Jette, who lives in a large house. Her mother is lying in bed behind a closed door.

"She's sick," says Jette.

"What's the matter with her?" I ask.

"She's depressed and takes pills for it," says Jette.

From behind the closed door, I can faintly hear a radio.

Jette has three siblings, two younger and one older, and they each have their own room. There's also a large living room and eat-in kitchen, although the kitchen table is completely covered with dirty dishes. "We're supposed to take turns washing up, but we always have an excuse for not doing it," says Jette as she washes two glasses so we can get something to drink. "Then Dad gets pissed when he comes home from work with grocery bags filled with stuff for dinner."

"I get it," I say.

Jette and I start spending every day together. I get money and cigarettes from Mom, and we're on our own at Jette's until her father gets home. I only see her mother a couple of times, usually when she has to go to the bathroom.

One day we go back to her house during lunch. We're out of cigarettes, so we try to find some at her place. We find a cigar in the liquor cabinet and light it up. Disgusting. I say we ought to wash the bad taste down with some of the booze in the cabinet. Jette gets two glasses and we start drinking from the different bottles. It's not something I'm used to, but we keep at it. Even though it tastes horrible, we're soon drunk. By the time we realize what time it is, next period has already started—and our schoolbags are still sitting in the classroom. We hurry off, dizzy and laughing up a storm.

We sneak into geography—and there's a substitute. Thank God. We stare down at our desks, certain that if the substitute looks in our eyes, she'll be able to tell we're drunk. I dare not look at Jette for fear that I'll start laughing. In a moment of inattention, I look over at her anyway, and she's sputtering with laughter. I quickly look away, and she regains control of herself. Every time I look over, she's stifling a laugh, which stops as soon as I look away. This goes on five or six times—until the substitute finally sends Jette out of the classroom for the rest of the period.

I start going to a motorcycle club in the center of Nakskov. Darius knows someone there, and he takes me with him a few times. On one of the first really warm spring days, they're throwing a party with music and dancing. It's a Friday, so I ask to spend the weekend at Mom's—that way I can do what I want.

There's plenty of booze and loud music. A young guy who introduces himself as Jens asks me if I want to dance. He looks okay. A little heavy with a crew cut, but his eyes are sweet. We dance together most of the night. He smells nice and I'm enjoying being close to him. Every so often, we stop to get a drink. Jens drinks beer, and so do I. Several hours have passed since I've seen Darius, but that doesn't matter. I have Jens. At one point, he kisses me gently while we're dancing. It's the first time I've ever kissed a guy. Later, he says he has to pee and asks me to wait for him while he goes outside.

A long time passes—at least half an hour. Now I'm looking for both Jens and Darius, but I don't see any sign of either of them. It's no fun anymore. A thin, black-haired guy in worn, dark clothes that seem a little too big for him comes over and asks who I'm looking for.

"Jens," I say. "Do you know him?"

"Oh yeah, Jens is one of my friends," he replies.

The guy seems to be in his early twenties. He says he just saw Jens outside and suggests we go out to look for him.

We walk out together into the darkness. He points at a small cluster of trees and bushes and says that's where he last saw him.

"Come," he says, taking my hand.

I don't like holding his hand. What if Jens sees me?

"Come on," he says, laughing as he pulls me away.

Where he takes me is dark and deserted, and I soon realize what's about to happen. He throws me down on the ground and puts his hand over my mouth while fumbling with his own pants and mine. I say no between his fingers, but he answers that I came on to him first and shouldn't act all high and mighty now.

I stop resisting. It's true: I foolishly went with him—and this is the price for my stupidity. My heart is pounding. I'm afraid he might kill me. If I just lie still . . .

He tears off my jeans and shoves hard into me, thrusting again and again, until he groans heavily and falls down on top of me, his mouth against my cheek. His breath is sour and hot, and I feel as if I'm going to vomit. My crotch is burning, and I'm crying silently from the pain. I stare up at the sky and count the stars, struggling to create systems out of them.

A moment later, he stands up, pulls on his pants, and runs off. I lie on the ground for a little while with dirt and branches in my hair and clothes. I look for my pants, but they're lying so far away that my hand can't reach them. I walk over to get my jeans and panties. My crotch and my abdomen are both sore. I dare not go back into the party.

Normally it takes a half hour to walk home to Mom and Richard's house, but tonight the walk feels like an eternity. Every step hurts, and I curse myself up and down for not taking my bike. The house is dark when I finally get there. I toss my pants and panties into the trash can and wash myself. The pain is unbearable. I crawl beneath the comforter, my knees up against my chest, knowing full well that I won't be getting any sleep.

That Sunday I go back to the orphanage, where Darius immediately asks where I got to on Friday.

"I did something really stupid," I say, winking as I smile.

Darius grins.

Before long, it's confirmation time at the orphanage. Those who aren't spending the weekend with their parents eat lunch in the living room with Mette and a temp social worker. Mette asks me to give the aviary an extra cleaning because of confirmation next week. I say no: I've cleaned it as many times as I should and I don't see any reason to clean it again. They'll have to get someone else to do it. Mette starts calling me lazy and says that I never want to do anything for anyone. I stand up and tell her to shut her mouth as I walk out of the living room. I slam the glass door so hard it rattles.

Before long, there's a loud knock on my door. It's Mette—and she's still yelling at me. I ask her to leave, but she keeps standing there; finally I take the chair I use to block the door and threaten to throw it at her. She leaves, but I'm so furious that I can't put the chair down. Instead, I throw it hard against the door, and the chair splinters into pieces, leaving a big mark on the door. I also toss the desk lamp at the door. It feels good.

Suddenly the door is almost kicked open—and Big Kim and Stig are standing there. They race in and each of them takes one of my arms. Mette stands there watching them. They drag me down the hall and into the bathroom, where they toss me on the floor of the shower and turn on the cold water. The whole section is there now, and they're all struggling to get a look.

The cold water is piercing, especially on my head, where it feels like nails against my scalp. Mette tells all of them to get out, turns off the water, and says that she hopes I've cooled off now.

"Real fucking smart, Mette," I yell hatefully, my teeth chattering. "Get the big boys to do your dirty work."

She stares at me for a moment and then walks out, closing the door behind her. I walk down to my room without looking up. I put on some dry clothes, jump out the window, and bike home to Mom. My teeth are chattering so loudly that people must be able to hear them as I ride past. No one is home, but I let myself in. I turn on the TV, lie down on the sofa, and wrap a comforter around me. Mom and Richard wake me up when they get home. It's dark outside now.

"What are you doing here?" asks Mom.

"I don't want to live in that shit hole anymore," I say.

"Well, you'll have to," she replies. "You certainly can't live here. I'm calling the orphanage right now and telling them you're sleeping here tonight but you'll be back tomorrow."

I don't respond. I don't have the strength to say anything else. She doesn't really understand at all.

As soon as I get back to the orphanage, I'm in a meeting again with the caseworker and both social workers, Jørgen and Anders, about my impossible and self-centered behavior. They tell me that Jørgen can't be my primary social worker anymore—from now on, it will be Anders. I ask why and am informed that Jørgen is taking a sabbatical. I stare into Jørgen's eyes. He's the only one I can even tolerate.

It's the spring of 1981. I'm thirteen, in eighth grade, and about to be confirmed. At the orphanage, I come and go as I please. Now and then I go home to see Mom or I stop at the bar where she and Richard hang out. The orphanage revokes my allowance whenever I do something I'm not supposed to, and they cancel my weekends with Holst and Dad, whom I've also started visiting. I don't care about the money—I can always get more from Mom—but it hurts to lose the weekends with Holst and Dad.

I ask to live with Dad, but they refuse; they say I'm so difficult that both Dad and the orphanage feel he can't handle me. They also accuse me of making irrational demands. I tell them that my only demand is to get the hell out of this shitty orphanage, yet they seem to want to punish me with staying whenever I want to leave. "That's not logical,"

I say, "just like all the other illogical and unintelligent crap you people come up with."

I'm informed that my confirmation party will be canceled if I don't start behaving. There's a month left. I've already invited the Holsts, Dad and Anita, and Mom and Richard—even though I know Richard won't come. He doesn't like parties. I've also invited my brothers and Richard's daughter, Bettina, who's living with another group in the same orphanage.

Mette has helped me pick out dresses for both my confirmation and the next day's parties, so everything is ready to go. We also planned our menu and table decoration—and even wrote our invitations together. Actually, it was a lot of fun doing all of it, though I sometimes wish I could do that kind of thing with Mom.

Now the orphanage wants to cancel all of it because of my behavior. I decide to put my best foot forward, at least until after my confirmation. I speak politely to the adults and offer to help when I see someone needs it. It's not easy, however, and I'm counting the days till my confirmation.

It turns out to be a lovely day. In church, Dad sits closest to me. He takes turns singing loudly from the hymnal and whispering that I should sit up straight. It's the first time the others in my class see Dad, and I'm proud of him. He's the handsomest father in the class.

My confirmation party was an important event for me, although the orphanage in Nakskov threatened to cancel it if I didn't start behaving. I managed to do so—until the very next day. What makes this photo special is that I look like a typical teenager with two happy parents. In reality, the confirmation party was held at the orphanage, where Mom and Dad arrived and left like all the other guests. The orphanage helped me buy confirmation clothes and prepare for the party. It was also the last time during our childhood that my brothers and I were all in one place.

The luncheon goes well. Mom and Dad sit on each side of me, and Dad gives a speech. He says that I've entered the adult world now and that I have to think about things and take responsibility for my actions. All the adults laugh loudly. I'm doing well in school, and I keep both my room and the aviary clean, so I don't know what he means.

I wish that Mom and Dad had helped with my preparations; instead, they arrive with all the other guests and leave at the same time. Most of all I enjoy being with Tonny, René, and Michael. I can't recall the last time we were all together. As soon as we see our chance, we get up from the table and walk down to my room, where Tonny and Michael smoke a joint. I take a few drags—it's the first time I try hash.

"Welcome to the adult world, sis!" says Tonny, and all three of us laugh loudly.

SKOLEPSYKOLOGISK RÅDGIVNING

KOPI

Storstrøms amtskommune
VESTLOLLAND

LIENLUND 4900 NAKSKOV (03) 92 14 88

NAKSKOV, den 01.04.1980.

LA/JA

Social- § Sundhedsforvaltningen
Ravnsborg kommune
Stationsvej 4
4913 Horslunde

MODTAGET

0 2.APR 1980

SO... FORVALTNINGEN
R...SBORG KOMMUNE

Vedr. Lisbeth Malene Zornig Andersen, f. 12.03.1968,
datter af Maja Jytte Nygaard, Bandholmvej 17B, 4943 Torrig

Efter Deres anmodning har jeg i forrige måned foretaget
klinisk psykologisk undersøgelse af Lisbeth:

Undersøgelsen, der har omfattet samtaler, intelligens- og per-
sonlighedstestning, viser Lisbeth som en godt begavet, tilsyneladende harmonisk og socialt særdeles veltilpasset pige.

Hun er imidlertid langt fra så problemfri, som hendes venligt
smilende fremtoning og fornuftigt omgængelige adfærd kunne lade tro.

Hun er ganske vist en pige med virkeligt gode muligheder for
selvstændigt og indlevende at opleve begivenheder, situationer og
mennesker omkring sig og til loyalt og ansvarligt at tage stilling
til og handle ud fra disse oplevelser.

Men hun er almindeligvis for ængstelig og utryg til at turde
bruge disse muligheder, hun har opfattet sin tilværelse og sine om-
givelser som så utilfredsstillende, skuffende og skræmmende, at det
har været uudholdeligt for hende at tænke, opleve og føle det så in-
tenst og dybt, som hun egentlig kan.

Hun har i stedet distanceret sig ved en tilsyneladende uanfæg-
tet, veltilpasset, men også noget overfladisk, farveløs, upersonlig
adfærd, og derved opbygget et værn mod oplevelsen af utryghed og
følelsesmæssig ensomhed, mod angsten for, hvad den nærmeste fremtid
måtte udsætte hende for.

Tilværelsen sammen med moderen har klart været meget belastende
for Lisbeth - sine barnlige (for alderen naturlige) behov for omsorg

- 2 -

og kærlighed oplever hun moderen som ligegyldig over for og en moden,
gensidigt forpligtende kontakt oplever hun moderen som for egoistisk
til at kunne indgå i.

Lisbeth ved om, ønsker og evner selv at indgå i følelsesmæssigt
nære og varige forhold mellem mennesker, men i sin hidtidige tilværelse
synes hun mest at have oplevet menneskelige relationer som overfladiske,
ustabile, udnyttende, ofte voldsomme og aggressive, særligt i forholdet
mellem mand og kvinde.

I samtale (NB efter, at jeg ud fra undersøgelsen har udtrykt som
min opfattelse, at det vil være bedst for hende ikke at skulle tilba-
ge til moderen) fortæller Lisbeth åbent om sin belastende tilværelse
sammen med moderen og udtrykker utvetydigt sit ønske om at leve ad-
skilt fra moderen, gerne en gang i en plejefamilie.

Lisbeth siger om moderen, at "hun er ikke så god til børn" og
sammenholder det med, at hendes tre brødre har fået det meget bedre,
efter at de er kommet hjemme fra, især ham, der er kommet i en rigtig god plejefamilie, der passer og interesserer sig for børn. Selv
har hun undertiden i dagevis opholdt sig alene i hjemmet sammen med
en jævnaldrende veninde uden tilstrækkeligt af mad og penge. Det
fremgår i det hele taget, at moderens livsførelse er særdeles uregel-
mæssig og uforudsigelig - forsømmelig, hvad angår hjemmets pasning,
opsyn med og omsorg for Lisbeth - i perioder præget af stort alkohol-
forbrug, værtshusbesøg, hvor Lisbeth har været taget med - ustabile
forhold til mænd med slagsmål og af moderen provokeret vold - økonomiske
smånumre og udnyttelse af andre.

Som en slags sammenfatning af, hvordan Lisbeth oplever forholdet
mellem moderen og sig selv, siger hun:" Det er ligesom, der er en skærm
mellem min mor og mig, som man ikke kan trænge igennem, vi har ikke
rigtigt noget sammen."

Vurdering af Lisbeths hidtidige tilværelse, aktuelle psykiske
tilstand og fremtidsudsigter:

Oplysninger fra socialforvaltningen og Lisbeths egne udtalelser
fortæller helt overensstemmende og i klar meningsfuld sammenhæng med tes
resultaterne om hjemmets udtalte mangel på ansvarlig voksen stabilitet
i livsførelse og følelsesmæssige relationer, i almindelig pasning af og
interesse for børn, i varm omsorg for og beskyttelse af børn ud fra
deres alder og behov. Ansvaret for Lisbeths pasning, opdragelse, følelsesmæssige og sociale tilpasning til tilværelsen har i hvert fald i de

*Shortly after my placement in the orphanage in Nakskov, Lars Algreen, the orphanage psychologist,
wrote a profile of me that became part of my case file. I remember my conversation with Lars quite
well. I told him that my relationship with Mom was a positive one. Lars evaluated me as functioning
normally and highly gifted, but also at risk for developing a neurosis as a result of serious neglect. At
one point, he observes: "Lisbeth is aware of, desires, and is capable of entering into emotionally close
and lasting relationships, but up until now she seems to have experienced human relationships as
superficial, unstable, exploitative, and often violent and aggressive, especially those between men and*

- 3 -

senere år stort set været hendes eget.

Lisbeth har vist stor psykisk styrke ved på denne baggrund at
have udviklet og overlevet med de gode personlige ressourcer, hun
rummer. Men som følge af det alt for store ansvar, hun har haft for
sin egen skæbne, har hun måttet forcere sig frem til en selvstændighed,
fornuftighed, social tilpasning, der i det lange løb både er skrøbelig og uhensigtsmæssig for hendes videre udvikling - skrøbelig, fordi
den personlige, følelsesmæssige modning ikke har kunnet holde trit
med den forcerede tilpasning - uhensigtsmæssig, fordi tilpasningen
er blevet et skjold mod og derfor også en hæmning for såvel barnlig
spontanitet og tryghedssøgen i voksnes omsorg som udfoldelse af dybere
(og dermed mere sårbare og risikobetonet)trang til på godt og ondt
at være sig selv i et følelsesmæssigt engageret forhold til omgivel-
serne.

Konklusion:

Det er allerede nu på høje tid at sikre, at Lisbeths gode per-
sonlighedsmæssige udviklingsmuligheder ikke bliver kvalt i et karak-
terneurotisk mønster, så meget mere som puberteten med dens fysiske
og psykiske omvæltninger er nært forestående. Varig anbringelse i familiepleje vil formentlig bedst tjene Lisbeths tarv.

Lars Algreen
klinisk psykolog

women." He concludes: "It's high time to ensure that Lisbeth's potential for personal development isn't
crushed in a typical pattern of neurosis, especially since puberty, with its physical and mental upheav-
als, is imminent. Lasting placement with a foster family would best serve Lisbeth's interests." Although
he recommended such placement, the orphanage ignored his recommendation. In my case files, the
orphanage writes that this profile was created when I was doing well but could not be used afterward
because it did not reflect reality. Reading the profile as an adult, I felt as if I were described exactly as
I still function today. He hit every mark.

1981–82

It's life as usual at the orphanage—and the conflicts only get worse. Anders is meeting with me now, but I miss Jørgen. We could argue, but there was always some warmth in his eyes. Not Anders. I feel like an animal being punished into doing the right thing, except it has the opposite effect. I keep asking to be placed with a foster family, but my request is rejected every time. Mom doesn't want that, and I'm too difficult.

I start saving to buy a train ticket to Copenhagen. I want to go there to live with my extended family, just like Michael, who kept running away from everywhere until they finally just gave up on him.

One Friday when I'm supposed to go to Holst's, I have enough money for the ticket. I pack a bag and tell the orphanage I'm taking the bus to Holst's, but instead I take the train to Copenhagen. At Central Station, I take the S-train to Brøndbyøster, where my Aunt Lis lives. I believe I can convince her not to rat on me. Michael has stayed there several times—that's where he met his girlfriend, and they're about to have twins. As I step off the train at Brøndbyøster station, my heart is pounding. What if she's not home or she's moved?

Carsten, her slow son, answers the door.

"Hello," he says, smiling.

Carsten and I are the same age, but he's a good foot taller. I don't think he recognizes me.

"Is your mother home?" I ask.

"Who is it, Carsten?" I hear Aunt Lis call from the living room.

"A girl," he replies.

"Come on in," yells Aunt Lis.

Carsten turns around to walk back into the living room, and I follow. Aunt Lis is lying on the sofa with a blanket wrapped around her, watching TV. Bowls of chips, bottles, and dirty clothes are all over the floor. The coffee table is covered with ashtrays and empty beer and soda bottles.

"Holy shit!" yells Aunt Lis. "It's Mouse. Come here and give your aunt a hug," she says, laughing, revealing her mouthful of black teeth.

Her hair is greasy and she smells like old liquor and fried food. I tell her I've run away from the orphanage and ask if I can stay with her.

"Of course, Mouse," she says. "You can sleep in the lower bunk, under Carsten."

I put my bag in Carsten's room. Toys and clothes are all over the floor; there's a comforter and a pillow on each bunk, but no sheets. And then there's that stench of fried food, alcohol, and cigarettes. Aunt Lis prattles on about what's on TV. I look around. Dirty dishes cover every surface in the kitchen, so I start to wash up. After that, I clean all the door handles so I can tolerate touching them, and then I clean the toilet in the bathroom.

Aunt Lis is happy; it's nice having someone clean up. At one point, she asks if I can also cut hair. I clip her bangs all the way up to her hairline. Carsten and I laugh out loud while she dashes into the bathroom to see what I've done—and then she laughs too.

After a few days with Aunt Lis, I realize that living here won't work. She has almost no money at all, and what she has she uses on takeout, cigarettes, and beer. I just can't tolerate Carsten, Aunt Lis, and her constant chatter about the TV.

On Sunday she takes me with her to Grandma and Grandpa's. It's wonderful to see them again. Several years have passed since I last saw them, but it feels like only yesterday. Grandma gives me some money for a ticket, and then Aunt Lis and I head for Central Station. She runs to catch the train back to Brøndbyøster, and I run to catch mine back to Nakskov and the orphanage. Fortunately, I don't have to wait long. Four hours later, I'm walking back into the orphanage, ready to receive yet another dressing-down, which oddly enough never happens. Instead, Anders is standing there, his face blank, telling me we need to have another meeting. I don't say anything; I just walk back to my room, set down my bag, and go out to find Darius.

At the same time, I'm informed that Jette will be going to a boarding school. I'm a bad influence on her. Jette, the only one in our class I see after school, understands me better than anyone. She knows how I function—that behind my defensive exterior I can laugh till the tears flow and offer a hug and that I really can feel something for other people. I just have trouble showing it in front of adults.

At the meeting with Anders, Grethe, and my mother, I'm told that the Holsts don't want to see me anymore. Anders says I've betrayed their trust. Normally I don't cry, but when Anders tells me that in his indifferent tone, the last part of the world I care about caves in.

I don't want to lose the Holsts—I never meant to hurt them. I sit for a long time fiddling with my glass. I realize I'm going to have to ask the orphanage for help. Cautiously, I ask if they would help me explain things to the Holsts—that I didn't mean them any harm and that they should continue to see me on the weekends.

"You should have thought of that before," says Anders.

I stand up without shouting, which I would normally do, and walk into my room, where I lie down on my bed and cry silently. I gave up expecting any adult to hear me a long time ago. I'm ashamed of having caused any problems for the Holsts, and I'm sad. Now I'm totally alone.

I lie there thinking about Ragna and her hot chocolate . . . about Holst and his typewriter . . . and about Troll.

Autumn of 1981 is a heavy time. The only people I'm speaking to at the orphanage are Darius and Kim Oskar. The adults and I avoid each other, and when we can't, it usually ends in a shouting match. I've decided to take care of what I have to and nothing else. I don't take walks with anyone, and I eat my meals in silence in the common room and leave as soon as I'm done. I avoid contact with anyone except Kim Oskar and Darius.

One day Kirsten calls me over. She's sitting in the small group of orange chairs just outside the living room. I walk over and she points at an obituary.

"Ragna Holst. Didn't you know her? She's dead now."

I take the newspaper and go back to my room. Yes, it's Ragna. What about Holst and Troll? What are they going to do without Ragna?

I walk back out and ask Kirsten what to do for a funeral. Kirsten says I can send a wreath to the church listed in the obituary; I just need to tell the florist the name of the church where Ragna will be buried. I ride my bike to the florist and ask if I can get a wreath for fifty kroner.

"What do you want on the card?" asks the florist.

"I don't know," I say. "Just write something and end it with 'warm greetings, Lisbeth.'"

I put the money on the counter and ride back to the orphanage.

A few weeks later, I get a card from Holst. My hands are shaking as I open the envelope. The card says: "Thank you for participating in our wife and mother's funeral service. Sincerely, Hans-Peder and Lars-Peder Holst." Really disappointing. A ridiculous thank-you card—with absolutely no indication that they even remember me.

Once again, I decide that I have to get away from the orphanage. My plan is to go to Copenhagen and live with Michael, who's eighteen now. The easiest path is through Dad, who has moved to Albertslund. I'm not allowed to see my brothers until we've all gotten a handle on our issues, so I can't get any help contacting Michael directly. It has to be done through Dad.

Both the orphanage and Mom agree to let me spend Christmas Eve with Dad and Anita. It's the first time I get to spend Christmas with them, and I'm sure it will be a wonderful evening. One of Anita's sisters is there with her kids, and Michael and his girlfriend, Pusser, are there too. I play with my three little half siblings, who are between one and eight years old. My half sister, Susan, is the sweetest little girl. I love tumbling around with the two boys and holding Susan, who laughs every time I do something goofy. All in all, I feel very comfortable with Dad and Anita.

They don't like my smoking, however, just as they don't like me visiting Michael so much. All through the holiday, I go to see Michael and Pusser in Brøndbyøster. I enjoy being with them and their twins, Anya and Betina, who are six months old. Both girls get the bottle, and I'm allowed to help feed them.

Every day, Michael and I shop at the Kvickly market near Nygårds Plads. Sometimes we start our little shopping trip by going to the top of the town's tallest building, which is at least ten floors, where we can sit undisturbed, staring out a window at Brøndbyøster. We smoke ourselves silly and talk about everything under the sun.

As we sit there talking, I feel happy and safe; I never want to go back to Lolland again. I want to live with Pusser and Michael and help with the twins. This is my real family. I tell that to Michael, who says it's okay. Afterward, we go down and shop: diapers, formula, and tons of baby food—and then candy and chips because we both have the munchies. Michael says that's common when you've smoked hash. We start eating before we even leave the store, all the while laughing and cheering. People stare at us, but I don't care.

Back at Michael and Pusser's, we put the food away while we play around. The twins sleep till noon in the bedroom. Michael grabs Pusser and starts dancing with her. Our giddiness rubs off on her, so the three of us decide to play feeding time while wearing blindfolds. We sit in a triangle on the floor, with a handkerchief wrapped around our eyes, each of us equipped with a spoon and three jars of baby food, and try to hit each other's mouths. I squeal with glee the first time I feel a spoonful of peas and carrots in my hair. It gets even funnier when, after we've emptied our jars, we take off our blindfolds and look at each other. There's baby food everywhere. Out of breath and happy, we sit there chuckling over having been so crazy.

That day, I go back to Dad and Anita's to tell them that Pusser and Michael have invited me to spend New Year's Eve with them. They've been invited by some friends and want me to come along. Dad and Anita say no. I explain that the twins are there, but Dad and Anita are opposed—they're sure I'll be offered booze and hash. Furious, I stop discussing it with them, pack my bags, and leave without saying goodbye.

I tell Michael and Pusser that I've left Dad and Anita and that I don't want to go back to Lolland. Michael says I can stay with them. Dad calls to talk to Michael, who tells him that I'm not coming back. A few hours later, Dad shows up to get me, but I refuse to go with him. I stare hatefully at him and tell him that maybe he should have thought about playing the responsible father a few years ago. It's a little late to start thinking that he, or any other adult, can make decisions for me. I'll be fourteen soon and I can manage on my own, as I've proven on several occasions. He's both hurt and angry. I don't care. He's been letting me rot in Lolland all this time—and he's repeatedly said no to having me live with him.

Dad stands up. He says goodbye, but I don't respond. I just stand there with my back to him. Furious. And feeling terribly sad, because it means I've lost yet another person in my life. But I'm not going to have him suddenly acting like he's my father.

On New Year's Day, the doorbell rings. When Michael opens the door, two police officers are standing there.

"Is Lisbeth Andersen staying at this address?" asks one of them.

"Yes," says Michael.

"Good. May we come in and talk to her?"

I can hear all of it from the living room. My heart is pounding. I'm sure someone must have died.

Michael and the two policemen come into the living room, where I'm sitting with one of the twins on my lap. They tell me I need to pack my things—that they're driving me back to Lolland.

"Why?" I ask.

"Because you've been reported missing," he replies.

I'm confused. How can I be missing when Dad and surely the whole orphanage knows where I'm staying? I'm getting angrier than I've ever been before. Do they think they can scare me by sending the police? Fucking cowards. I stand up, my eyes filled with angry tears, hand the baby to Pusser, and go to pack my bag. I give each of the twins a kiss on the forehead. Michael and Pusser are waiting in the hall, and they both give me a hug. Pusser has tears in her eyes; Michael's are stone cold and dark. He's pissed. The silent policeman takes my bag, and then they take me by the arms and almost lift me down the front steps.

Two small boys, each about eight years old, are standing out front waiting. When they see me with two large policemen on either side of me, one of them exclaims: "See—the police are taking her." I put my bag in the back of the police car that will take me back to Nakskov. The policemen walk me all the way into Family Group, and the boys who are home crowd around me to hear what I've done. Anders is there too.

I squeeze through the crowd to get to my room, where I slam the door shut. There's a knock on the door.

"Can I come in?" asks Darius.

"Come on in," I answer.

I'm trying to figure out what to take with me. I've decided to go home to be with Mom and Richard.

"What have you done now, Lisbeth?" he asks.

"My father wouldn't let me see my brother," I say, "but he shouldn't decide that—so I visited him anyway. Then they sent the cops after me. As if that was going to scare me. Do you want to go with me to Mom and Richard's? I'm pretty sure they're at the Lido."

"Okay," he says and then goes to get his jacket.

We walk out through the dorms so we avoid the policemen and Anders, who are standing by the main entrance.

The next day, I participate in a special meeting to determine what will happen to me, which isn't exactly a surprise, given what's been happening. All the powers that be are present. I'm informed that the orphanage can't do anything else for me. In addition, Mom wants me placed far enough away from her that I can't just show up there whenever it suits me. I stare indifferently around the room, smoking all the while.

Suddenly I hear Mom saying that I've made a pass at Richard and that's why I need to be far away. Confused, I stare at her, but then I realize what's happening. Richard and I have been talking more and more frequently about different things, and she feels left out. It might even be the news we're watching together; he plays cards with me a lot too. To put it simply, I'm becoming a threat—a young woman who's competition now. I need to be disposed of so she can have Richard all to herself. As usual, she's convinced the orphanage that she's the victim who needs help. On more than one occasion, I've been told that I'm taking advantage of Mom. Jesus, they're blind and stupid.

They decide they need to find me an orphanage that's far away. Also, I need a relief family I can stay with in Nakskov when Mom can't handle having me there on weekends.

I go on spending weekends with Mom until I have to move to Hylleholt Residence for Girls, which has a spot for me right after my fourteenth birthday, in February of 1982. A month before my departure, Mom has a falling-out with Richard. This time she decides to leave him; one of her friends at the bar lets her stay at his tiny house in Lindet while she's waiting for an apartment from the township.

The house consists of one room with a hot plate in the hallway, a bathroom with a sink, and a loft. I spend only one weekend there and soon realize the owner expects sexual favors from Mom as rent. One night I hear him sneaking into the house. He pulls off his pants and lifts up Mom's comforter. She doesn't say a word. At some point, I look over the edge of the loft. Mom's in pain: her eyes are shut tight and she's biting her lower lip. The man is lying on top of her, humping away, until he reaches orgasm. Then he gets up, dries himself off with a roll of toilet paper that's on the table, and slips out the door. I'm livid. I'm furious with him and think it's terrible for Mom, but I decide to act like nothing has happened so she won't be embarrassed.

The next day, Mom and I are at the Iron Rod with a few of her friends. They tell us there's a new discotheque in Kragenæs, and we decide to drive over. There's a disco ball on the ceiling, strobe lights in many colors, and a stripper pole on stage. It's amazing. The music is loud and they're playing all the latest hits.

We're having a lot of fun—and there's free Malibu rum for everyone because it just came on the market. I drink it too, even though I don't like the taste of coconut. Some young guys are making a lot of noise, and one of them keeps staring at me. A thin guy with mid-length blond hair and freckles, he has large, crooked front teeth. At one point, he comes over and asks if I want to dance. They're playing Laban's "Where Should We Sleep Tonight?" It's a big hit, so the dance floor is already full.

He grabs my hand as we walk out onto the dance floor. We dance really close, even though it's not that kind of song. He says his name is Niels; he's eighteen and learning to be a carpenter. He smells wonderful. "It's my deodorant—Rexona," he replies when I ask what he's wearing. "The brown one," he adds.

We keep dancing till they finish playing the last song. "Have a good night, everyone," I hear over the loudspeakers as I pull him even closer. His smell, the music, and the Malibu have made me woozy and happy. I don't want the night to end.

Right before the song ends, he kisses me, gently and with his lips closed, and then he looks at me inquisitively. I tilt my head back and turn my face up toward his. He kisses me again, this time a little more intensely, but with his lips still closed. My whole body is whirring and buzzing. I want the moment to last forever. The music ends, though, and the lights come on. We walk over to Mom's table, where everyone's about to stand up.

"Why don't we go back to my place for a little party?" asks Mom.

I look at Niels, who then looks at his friends, who've moved over toward Mom's table. They say they're tired and want to head home.

But Niels says, "Sounds good."

I feel a rush of joy.

A couple of Mom's bar friends take a taxi with us back to the tiny house. We bought some beer at the disco, and when we get home, everyone gets one. I can barely drink. I'm nauseated and tired—and I'm not sure what to do with Niels. I'd like to go to sleep, and I want him to stay, but I don't know how to say it.

The problem solves itself when Niels asks if we should go up to the loft to talk. "Yes!" I exclaim a little too loudly. I hurry off to pee and wash myself. I realize this will probably end in sex, but I'm not afraid.

His smell, his eyes, his hands, and, crazy as it seems, his teeth are so appealing.

By the time I climb the ladder to the loft, he's waiting, naked, beneath my comforter. I can hear the others talking and laughing below. I lie down next to him with all my clothes on. Slowly he takes them off while staring into my eyes. His eyes seem to be asking for permission. My heart is pounding, and my hands are clammy and cold. I don't know what he expects, so I don't do anything, other than lifting myself up a little when he has trouble getting something off me. Finally he pulls off my panties and lies down next to me while he tucks the comforter around both of us. Most of the time he's staring into my eyes. Asking silently. I don't say a word. Just stare back. My whole body is flexing.

We lie there holding each other for a long time. I can feel his stiff penis against my thigh, but he's not pressuring me. Just lying there waiting. Staring inquisitively into my eyes. I don't know how long we lie like that. Maybe an hour. Anyway, it's quiet downstairs now, except for my mother's faint snoring. My body is getting warmer and warmer, as if I'm thawing, and I'm warm and moist. I want Niels to make love to me, but he doesn't do anything. I take one of his hands and place it between my legs, so he can tell that I want him. He gently pushes me onto my back, spreads my legs a little, pulls the comforter down over both of us, and slowly penetrates me. It hurts a little. The whole time, he's looking at me while moving slowly. A moment later, he pulls out again. He turns me around so I'm lying on my side, lies down behind me with one arm under my head and the other around my chest, and then kisses my neck and says, "Good night."

When I wake up late the next day, he's still holding me the same way. He's awake. He smiles and says good morning.

"Good morning," I say.

"Would you like to come home with me today to see where I live?" he asks.

"Sure," I say, beaming with joy.

"Good. I'll come by to get you later on my moped. I have to go home first. I need to help my father with a few things," he says.

Niels is my first real boyfriend. Just as I'm about to say goodbye to Lolland, eighteen-year-old Niels suddenly pops up. My hard shell dissolves slowly in his love and desire. I enjoy every minute we're together, and I try to arrange all the days before my departure so we can be together. We spend most of the time beneath the comforter. I feel as if I'm soaking up all his energy when we're lying close. The lovemaking is nice and gentle, but it's even more important just to lie that close.

We usually make love in Niels's parents' home. His mother is a housewife, and his father is a painter. They're fine with me coming over—although I don't speak to them when they're there—and they always set a place for me at each meal. Aside from that, we spend all our time in Niels's room; when we're not there, we're riding around on his moped with his friends. I sit behind him, holding his waist and happily going wherever he takes me. It doesn't matter where we are, as long as we're together.

Just before I leave for Faxe Ladeplads, I'm introduced to Birthe and Johannes Palshøj, who'll be my relief family after I move. They live in a white house with a large garden on the border of Nakskov and have three children: Søren, Peter, and Karen-Lise. Peter is grown, though, and doesn't live at home. Søren is a few years older than me, and Karen-Lise is my age. She's the only one of the three children who is home that day.

I sit there studying her on the sly. She's tall and has short strawberry-blonde hair, a slightly pointy face, and sorrowful eyes. She says that she sings with the choir in church. Birthe, who has short dark hair and is about forty and a bit chunky, tells me that they go to church every Sunday and that I'm welcome to come along.

"No, thanks," I say, smiling wryly.

Birthe asks about my interests.

"Reading and metal shop," I say.

Birthe says they have a lot of books I can borrow.

"Great," I say, lighting up a cigarette.

Johannes, Birthe's husband, doesn't say much. He just sits back listening while he smokes a cigar. He's tall and thin and has freckles all over; the little bit of hair left on his head is strawberry blond, just like Karen-Lise's.

We talk a little about how often I should stay with them. We agree to start with once a month—they'll get double fostering allowance for that—and then we take off. I need to go home and pack my things so I'll be ready for my last ride in the orphanage's bus. I can't wait. I don't see moving far away from Niels as such a big problem. I plan to come back to Nakskov every weekend, staying either at Mom's or at the Palshøjs', so we can definitely see each other at either place.

1982–83

Once again I find myself sitting in the orphanage bus. Saying goodbye to Niels was tough. I cried bitterly when I kissed him goodbye the day before, and he cried too. Damn. I hope I'll be back in Nakskov for a weekend soon so I can see him again. He's the best thing that's ever happened to me—and here I am on a bus headed for a totally different part of the country.

It was tough saying goodbye to Grethe too. She gave me a big hug at school yesterday. It wasn't easy holding back my tears, but I did. It would have been horrible if the others had seen me wailing. Especially Steen and Allan. Fucking idiots. I'm not sad about leaving them.

I lean back and start counting the street signs and trees. I suddenly realize that I rarely ever count anymore. God knows when it stopped. I still look for ghosts under the bed and in the closets in a certain order, but I can control it. Not counting anymore is fantastic.

It reminds me of the day I discovered the warts on my hands were gone. In the middle of a meal, I happened to glance down at my hands. The warts were gone, and all that was left were a few scars on one pinkie. I hadn't been treated for them or anything. They were just gone.

We arrive in Faxe Ladeplads, and Anders parks the bus in the school's parking lot. The house, which is located in the middle of an old residential area, is a kind of overgrown villa with pale-yellow walls and brown windows with mullions.

We ring the doorbell, and a moment later, a short, wide, dark-haired woman in her fifties wearing a brightly colored dress opens the door. She's grinning from ear to ear, and her eyes crinkle up so much that I can't see their color. I can tell that she once had a cleft lip.

"Hello, hello," she exclaims loudly in her singsong Jutland accent. "You must be Lisbeth," she adds, taking my hand. "I'm Rigmor, and I'm the principal here. I've really been looking forward to meeting you."

She looks me right in the eye—she really does seem happy to see me. She leads me into her office, where she turns to Anders and extends her hand.

We sit in some easy chairs surrounding a low, round conference table in the corner of the office. I barely sit down before the door opens and yet another happy-faced, though somewhat younger, woman enters. She walks over and shakes my hand. "Britt," she says, staring into my eyes while smiling. She's short too, but thin and unbelievably pretty. The social workers are really small here, I think. Britt and Rigmor tell me a little more about themselves. Rigmor says that she lives at the school in an apartment on the second floor; she's not married and has no children. On the other hand, she has a poodle named Pigro, whom all of us can pet and take for walks if we want to. Britt, who says she has a daughter, lives in a large house with her sister and her husband.

Rigmor and Britt ask me a lot of questions. They barely speak to Anders. They talk about the school's daily routines: We get up at the same time every day, and then we clean up a designated area before breakfast, which is also served at a set time. Then it's time for school. At first I have to go to the in-house schoolroom, but then Hylleholt will determine if I'm ready to start at the local public school. After school there's kitchen duty and set times for homework and cleaning your room. There's also yoga, Jane Fonda exercises, and personal care, which means that every Friday we get our nails done on both our hands and feet. Bedtime is also at a fixed time. Every night, Rigmor goes around to all the rooms, closes the curtains, and checks that we're ready for bed. Afterward, a night nurse comes in to chat for a while and give us a hug while tucking us in.

Rigmor tells Anders to go so that she and Britt can show me around. "Say goodbye to Anders now, Lisbeth, so we can take a tour around the house. Anders, you can just toss Lisbeth's things here in the hallway before you leave." After Anders shakes Rigmor's and Britt's hands, I walk with him out into the hallway.

"Well, this is goodbye, Lisbeth," Anders says.

He leans down and gives me a gentle hug.

"So long, Anders," I say. "No need to tell those fools down there I said hello." I smile.

He smiles in return, and I walk back into the office.

Britt and Rigmor show me around the entire house. There are two sitting rooms. You can't smoke in one of them, but a group of girls is sitting around talking and smoking in the other. Two of them are playing the board game Kalah, and another is playing a pedal organ. It doesn't sound very good, though it looks like fun.

"Say hello to Lisbeth," says Rigmor.

Half of the girls look up and say hi. The rest keep doing what they're doing.

"We say hello to our houseguests here," Rigmor says loudly in a stern voice—and then everyone looks up and says hello.

We walk through the large dining hall, which has a number of tables, each with room for four. There are flowers in all the vases and pots, beautiful curtains, and art on the walls. Rigmor sees me staring at the paintings.

"We borrow the art from an art library," she says. "It should be just as lovely as any private home here—it's important to us."

And it is lovely. Everything is well maintained, clean, and orderly. The school also has a lounge, a sewing room, a dance studio, and a laundry room—and then there's the classroom, a cozy room up on the very top floor. We end the tour at the dormitory hall, where I get to see my room. I'll have to live in a triple at first.

"That's how everyone starts," says Rigmor. "It's a good way to get to know the others." She also tells me that soon I'll get my own room. For now, I'll have to share the triple with someone named Tina, who's just moved in.

"Hi," says Tina, smiling at me as we enter.

"Hi," I reply. She looks sweet. The third bed is empty.

Britt hasn't said much during the tour; mostly she's been handing out hugs and comments to the girls we've encountered along the way.

"Britt, can you help Lisbeth get settled in?" asks Rigmor.

Britt and I go back down to get my things in the hallway so I can unpack. My bed is already made with floral-patterned sheets. Britt asks if I have a boyfriend.

"Yes," I reply. "Niels."

"He must be a real sweetheart," she says. "If you want to, you can call him from the office and tell him you've arrived safe and sound."

I feel as if I fit in better here than anywhere else I've been. I like the daily routines, and the other girls seem nice. I'm left in peace without feeling neglected. Just the way I like it. All meals are at a set time—there's barely an hour in the day that isn't filled with some activity. I have to stay at the school the first weekend I'm there, to get to know the place a little better, but then I can spend weekends at home with the Palshøjs or Mom. My decision.

I take the days as they come and don't think about Niels that often. I don't even give Mom a thought. I spend the first weekend exploring Faxe Ladeplads. It's a small town with a lot of vacation homes, an inn, a hotel, a bookstore, a butcher, a newspaper kiosk, a perfumery, a bakery, and two supermarkets. There's also a small station with a train that goes to Køge. I haven't been in Køge since Dad lived there. I haven't heard a word from him since the police came to get me; I really don't want any contact with someone who would send the police after me.

The days fly by, and soon it's time to spend a weekend in Nakskov. I sit on the steps of Gefion, the local inn, waiting for the bus. All set with my birth control pills, a bag of clean clothes, and polished nails on both my hands and feet. The other girls who also live in Nakskov are going to show me how to get there.

I stay close to Alice, who's a few years older than me. I have no idea why she's at Hylleholt; she seems totally healthy, normal, and rational. During the train ride, we agree that I'll visit her at her parents' home in Nakskov.

As the train pulls into Nakskov, I see Niels waiting anxiously at the station. Even though we haven't seen each other in two weeks, I've barely had time to miss him. The social workers at Hylleholt were sweet to let me call him now and then.

Niels, in worn jeans and a black leather jacket, is holding a crash helmet and grinning from ear to ear, so I can see all his teeth. I'm wearing the same giddy smile until the train stops and the doors open.

Alice departs first. Her parents and little brother and sister have come to get her. Then it's my turn. Niels steps onto the train and grabs my white Adidas sports bag, the one I got from the orphanage when I started taking self-defense classes several years ago. He sets it down on the platform. I'm barely out of the train before he puts his arms around me, lifts me up, and swings me around while we laugh.

Setting me down, he stares into my eyes in that special way, as if he's searching for something and has all the time in the world to find it. And then he kisses me. Again and again. He knows I don't like French kissing, so he kisses me with his mouth closed, slow, warm, safe kisses that make my heart settle down. Like a small dog, I follow him to his moped, and we ride to Mom's apartment.

Mom's home. I can hear the TV as we open the door at the foot of the stairs. This is the oldest part of Nakskov: the houses are yellow and lopsided with visible half timbering. At street level, there's a narrow door leading up to Mom's apartment.

I hesitate at the door to her apartment. For a moment, I wonder if I should knock. I grab the door handle and slowly open the door. From the entrance, I can see Richard's feet on a footstool. So he's there too. I feel like slipping back out again, but that might seem weird to Niels, so I open the door, yell "Hi," and walk in with Niels behind me.

The apartment is dark and musty. There are several days of dirty dishes lying around and a frying pan with caked-on grease on the stove.

"Hi," Mom yells back. "We're in the living room."

"Hi," I say again.

"Hi," says Richard without looking up from the TV.

Mom stands up nervously. "Let me get you a couple of cups for coffee."

She seems jumpy; something is wrong. I'm sure we've walked into the middle of something that will end in a scuffle between her and Richard.

"No, don't bother," I say. "I just wanted to say hello. I'll be staying with Niels this weekend. We'll stop in again tomorrow."

"Sounds like a plan," says Mom, clearly relieved. "I can make dinner tomorrow—maybe beef stew?"

"Sounds good," I say and turn to leave.

Niels looks confused. On the way down the stairs, he asks if I shouldn't spend a little time with my mother since I've come home to be with her this weekend.

"No," I reply. I haven't missed her—and she seems more relieved than disappointed that I left so abruptly.

"What do you think Hylleholt's going to say when they hear you haven't slept at your mother's?" he asks.

"Who's going to tell them—Mom? After a few days, she'll forget everything about it, and anyway she couldn't care less. That's clear to everyone."

We ride to Niels's home in Vesterborg and go straight up to his room. He slowly takes off all my clothes, lays me down on his bed, and wraps his black comforter around me. He undresses quickly and slips beneath the comforter. We lie there for a long time, completely silent, just sensing each other's presence.

As usual, I'm cold all over; my hands are clammy, and my toes are icy, whereas he's warm and dry. I move in as close as possible, so that my whole body is touching his. Almost clinging to him, I get that feeling of sapping him of something. The warmth spreads quietly inside me, my body slowly relaxing.

Just as quietly, he starts to kiss my neck and breasts, moving farther down to my stomach. I tense up again. He's moving down to lick me, and I don't want that. Memories of Jan and Stig start to surface, and I'm about to panic.

"What's wrong, Lisbeth?" he whispers.

"I don't want you to do that," I whisper back.

He lies still for a little while until my body relaxes and once again I'm warm. He starts kissing my stomach again, moving his tongue in a circle as he gets closer. Now and then he looks up to see how I'm reacting. I lean back and close my eyes, putting my hands on his head and pushing him down farther. Inside, I feel a great rage, but somewhere in the middle of all my fear there's a light. I let him do it, stifling the urge to shove him away. He licks for only a moment, and then moves up on top of me again, kissing my mouth and my cheeks. I can smell myself on his mouth.

"I'm so happy you're my girlfriend," he whispers in my ear.

And I'm happy you're my boyfriend, I think.

The only time I see Mom that weekend is Saturday evening, when Niels and I go there for dinner. Richard's there too, and Mom flutters nervously around him, all the while babbling, trying to get him to talk and participate. But Richard says nothing. Now and then he grunts—but that's about it. I don't say anything either. I just sit there watching the entire dinner scene, which occurs at the coffee table with the TV on. It's entertaining enough to watch Mom and Richard eating.

Mom puts potatoes and beef stew on Richard's plate first and cuts the potatoes for him. Then she put some on her own plate. Richard grabs his fork and starts shoveling the food in quickly and systematically. Finally he turns his easy chair away from the table and watches a little TV before falling asleep. Mom cuts her own potatoes and then mashes them up until they resemble baby food, all the while chattering away.

It's like she has to say every thought that comes into her head. We get a detailed description of how she mashes up the potatoes and mixes in the sauce. And she repeats it several times while her right hand energetically demonstrates everything. There's a little quiet while she's eating, but as soon as she's done, she starts up again. Then she tells us— three times—why she's not doing the dishes until tomorrow.

I don't know how Richard tolerates her constant chatter. Maybe he's developed an ability to stay inside his own head so he doesn't hear it. It would explain why he doesn't answer when she asks him something.

I barely understand Mom—and she barely understands me. Communication between us is quite simplistic. If I tell her I got a B on an essay, she'll tell me she got a new refrigerator. She's not being malicious. I think she just makes a connection between the fact that I've gotten something with her getting something. She doesn't grasp that I want her to be proud of me. We're not on the same wavelength.

And she's afraid of me. Afraid of what I might say. Sometimes, when she says something so stupid it makes my head spin, I don't even answer her. At other times, I tell her she has the IQ of the chickens we used to chop the heads off in Nordlunde. The way I snap at her makes her frightened and nervous.

I can't wait to get away from Mom's apartment and go home with Niels; as soon as we're done eating, we leave. On Sunday afternoon, Niels drives me to the train station. When I get back, I'll be starting at the local public school, so it's not that hard to say goodbye to him.

Smoking and aloof, I'm wearing a very masculine expression in this photo from Hylleholt Residence for Girls.

Back at Hylleholt, it's a lovefest. In the evening, we have rolls and juice, and everyone speaks in excited tones. Several of the girls act as if they haven't seen each other in months, and the social workers are handing out hugs left and right. It reminds me of a family that's been away from each other for a long time—like the few times my brothers and I have reunited. We get so giddy when we're together, and then we tease Mom, who laughs although she has no idea what we're talking about.

On Monday I start at my new school. My homeroom teacher's name is Børge, and he's married to Karen, a social worker at Hylleholt. She's on sabbatical right now, so I haven't met her. Børge is tall and thin, with a full beard and dark, curly, midlength hair. He's probably around forty. He always wears a green cap with a Red Army star on it, and mandarin-collar shirts in different colors. There's no talking in his classes, but during our free periods, he hangs out with us. I've never had this type of teacher before; he acts like one of us between classes and is willing to talk to us about anything—and if one of us gets hurt or sad for whatever reason, he gives us a hug and comforts us.

In class, though, he's tough and ambitious. He gives a ton of homework and expects a lot from us. And God help you if you haven't done it—you really get chewed out. Everyone wants to make Børge proud, so we work our asses off for even the slightest compliment. It's not about getting an A—it's about making the effort.

Børge quickly picks up on my skills in Danish. If I make a mistake in dictation or a grammar error in my Danish essays, he calls me out and tells me to take my head out of my ass. To stop thinking about boys for one second and concentrate. I don't get angry or afraid—it just makes me want to do better.

Børge introduces me to all kinds of literature, including Alex Haley's *Roots*. He also wants us to be familiar with the Danish classics, from Johannes V. Jensen to Klaus Rifbjerg to Leif Panduro, and I can't get enough of it. When I discover there's this thing called apartheid,

Børge encourages me to write an essay about it. He's impressed by the fact that I'm interested in marginalized social groups.

Fatina is the only one in Danish class who's at my level. She and I spend the first few days sizing each other up. Fatina is obviously the class babe—and all the boys love her. She's dark and beautiful, with curves in all the right places, and she's luminous in every way. Fatina is the result of a love affair between a Syrian father and a Danish mother who's a high school teacher.

The second youngest of eight children, Fatina's a rebel. She knows how to work the boys and men, who fawn all over her. She also writes the most wonderful and imaginative essays, which she always gets the highest grade for, and she's a divine artist. Somehow we latch on to each other, and within a few days, we're inseparable. It's like a romantic relationship. We're together every day after school—they have to almost toss her out of Hylleholt when it's time to go to bed. On the weekends when I don't go back to Nakskov, we sleep together, and sometimes I take her with me when I'm staying with the Palshøjs. They're happy for me at Hylleholt, and they encourage the friendship.

I have a serious problem with German. I'm taking advanced courses in all my subjects—including German—but in one of my first German classes, the teacher, Kubel, asks me to decline a noun. The problem is that I don't know what a declension is.

"I don't understand," I say.

He looks at me for a long time and says: "If you can't do something this elementary, then you need to move down a level." I sense those old feelings swelling within me. Hate. Fear. Loneliness. I stand up slowly and start gathering my things. The class is completely quiet. The other students are staring at me—and so is Kubel. I don't think he knows what to say.

"What are you doing?" he asks.

I don't respond. I finish packing my things, grab my bag, and slip out the door. I'm done with German. I don't say anything about it when I get back to Hylleholt. I sneak up to my room without being seen and lie down on my bed. My whole world is falling apart. I made a mistake. The adults in Faxe Ladeplads are all assholes too.

A few hours later, Britt comes into my room and sits down on the edge of the bed.

"The school called," she says, stroking my hair.

I don't respond.

"Rigmor has asked Kubel to come to a meeting so we can talk about what happened."

"I'm not going to any meeting," I say, turning to face the wall. "I'm done with German and that idiot teacher."

"What happened?" asks Britt.

I tell her what he said to me.

"Yes, that sounds incredibly stupid."

I start to cry while Britt holds me.

A few days later, I have a meeting with Kubel and Rigmor. Kubel starts by apologizing for his foolish remark. I don't say anything; I just stare down at the table. Then Rigmor asks if there's anything the school can do to help me get to the same level as the others in German.

"Yes," says Kubel. "If you'd like, Lisbeth, you can come to my place a couple of times a week for a little extra instruction."

I think he really means it.

"Okay," I say.

We agree on a time for my first tutoring session, and then Kubel shakes our hands before leaving. I'm both confused and relieved: I've never experienced a solution like this before.

I take up rowing. Britt, who belongs to a club, helps me get involved. Dorthe from my class rows too, although she's much better than I am.

She's even rowed in regattas with some of the others from school. I'm afraid of water—well, actually, of what's beneath it—which isn't smart when you have to row several hundred yards out from the coast. We reach a compromise: they put me in one of the old boats where I'm one of four rowers with a coxswain, and everyone has an oar. It feels somewhat safer, especially when you're wearing a life vest.

Once I overcome my fear of water, I start to enjoy the rowing excursions. The calm and the sound of the water as our oars glide through it are wonderful. I don't talk much to the other rowers, but they don't seem to mind. After a while, they let me become a coxswain, which is amazing. As coxswain, I get to say whether or not they're rowing out of synch. I enjoy that. Being coxswain is one of the best things about rowing.

Parents Day at Hylleholt arrives in May. Although Mom was invited, she hasn't responded. It will be fun to see the other girls' families; both siblings and parents are coming. Soon the house is crammed full of people talking and eating. There are guided tours of the rooms, and we're all wearing our finest clothes. A few of the other girls and I sewed some of the clothes. Rigmor calls Mom to ask if she is coming, but she says she can't RSVP before finding out if she has enough money to make the trip. Apparently she doesn't because she never shows up. I really wanted to show her the place and my room; instead, I'm the only one who has no visitors. None of the other girls or parents act as if they even notice. Rigmor keeps an eye on me, though, and despite all those parents who want to talk, she manages to come over and give my arm a little squeeze. This small gesture helps me stay all afternoon; I even lend a hand in the kitchen when the whole family idyll becomes a little too oppressive.

Rowing, extra German classes, homework, and Fatina fill my days—
but there are also all the household chores we have to take care of at
Hylleholt. Every morning, between 7:15 and 7:30, each of us has an
area we have to clean before we can eat breakfast and go to school. The
whole house buzzes with activity: you can hear vacuum cleaners and
toilet brushes all over the place. Everyone works fast so we can go down
to eat breakfast. We also have our weekly Wednesday cleaning, which
takes all afternoon, when we straighten up our own rooms plus one of
the common areas. On top of that there's weekly laundry. Finally there's
weekly food prep, which starts right after I get home from school. We
have to make food for twenty people, and it's all made from scratch.

Two of us work on food prep during each shift, along with the kitchen
manager, Øster, who's always in a white smock. Thin and gray haired,
she has light-blue eyes and a shiny white smile. Øster teaches me the
chemistry behind the food. She says if you understand how ingredients
work, both individually and together, under hot and cold conditions,
you can avoid using a cookbook. I love making food with her; basically,
I just love making food, so the kitchen soon becomes my favorite place
to be. We meet there every day after school at the kitchen counter with
the tall stools for buns, tea, and juice. All afternoon, a steady parade of
girls stops by to grab something to eat or chat with one of the adults
sitting there.

In the dining hall, we're four to a table—and each of us has a cloth
napkin, which sits inside a cloth sleeve that has our number on it. We
have assigned seats, so our napkins are always there, along with the rest
of our place setting. Whoever's making the food also has to serve it. We
serve from the left, and if there are several courses and plates have to be
removed during the meal, we take them from the right. Rigmor says we
need to learn how to behave everywhere—even among the upper crust.

One day the curtains have to be washed. It's one of those days when I'm both rowing and taking my extra German class—and no one has told me I have to take down my curtains this afternoon before I can go anywhere. At breakfast, Rigmor tells us to take down our curtains when we get home from school.

"I don't have time for that," I say.

"Of course you do," replies Rigmor.

I feel the storm clouds gathering overhead, the same old clouds that I don't want there but that I can't get to dissipate. I try arguing that I have a tight schedule in the afternoons, but Rigmor interrupts me and says that she wasn't asking a question. It's a chore I have to do, just like all the others.

I stand up so abruptly that I knock over my chair; then I storm out without looking at her while trying to control the ire that's about to make my head explode. I don't want this. I don't want any conflicts, but I can't accept unexpected orders at the breakfast table when I've already planned my day.

I slam the door to the back hallway and stomp up to my room, where I grab my bag and then march furiously to school. Rigmor lets me go, but that afternoon she's standing there like a hawk when I come home to fetch my sweat suit.

"Lisbeth," she says, standing in my doorway, "we need to talk."

I scowl at her as I pull down the curtains.

"There's no point in planning your days so that nothing unforeseen can happen. Once you finally leave here, you're going to encounter a lot of unexpected things—and you have to learn how to deal with them."

I know what she means. I'm at my best when I know exactly what's happening every minute of the day. When my plans get interrupted, it sends me into a tailspin.

"Also, Lisbeth, the way you're behaving lately seems totally self-absorbed to everyone else. You're on overdrive every day, which means you have no time left to talk to anyone or enjoy yourself. The others feel as if you don't really care about them," she continues.

That's just the way I am, I think, though I don't say it.

"I'd like you to speak to our psychologist," she says. "I think your full schedule is an attempt to repress something—a fear, a loss, or something you need to work through. I know full well that you aren't self-absorbed, and I know how much you care about the adults here and what a good friend you are. And your seeming indifference toward others is surely a smoke screen for something else, something you need help with. I think our psychologist, Anne-Marie, can help you with that."

"Okay," I say.

"Good," says Rigmor, flashing me one of those big grins that make her eyes disappear into her face. And then she leaves.

So, I start attending sessions with Anne-Marie, who wants me to tell her all about my experiences. Which I have no intention of doing. Rigmor can force me into the same room with a psychologist, but I decide whether or not I'm going to speak to her. I've brought along a nail file: my nails are starting to look really nice since I've stopped biting them.

Anne-Marie's trying, but I don't really know her that well. I'd never be able to tell her about Mogens, Jan, Stig, the rape, those long nights lying awake in the house in Torrig, and all those fights. I wouldn't even be able to tell Rigmor, Britt, or Niels, so how in the world would I tell some woman I barely know?

I meet with Anne-Marie a couple of times, but I just sit there, filing away and saying nothing. After a few sessions, Rigmor, smiling wryly, suggests that we stop the therapy sessions. And I'm allowed to go on with my tight schedule, which suits me just fine.

The weekends in Nakskov are very different, depending on whether I'm staying with the Palshøjs or Mom. When I'm at Mom's, I spend most of my time with Niels. The Palshøjs are stricter about when I can see Niels. I don't talk much when I'm with them; most of the time, I just lie in my room and read, or I borrow a bike and ride into town to see Mom at the Lido (or wherever she is that day).

Sometimes I tell Niels that the Palshøjs won't let me see him, even though it isn't true. I'm starting to get tired of him. We do the same thing every time we're together. My need to cuddle has dwindled considerably since I've been at Hylleholt; I'd rather read than ride around on his moped and drink beer with his friends. Still, Niels is really sweet, and I don't have the heart to tell him I'm bored.

Soon it's summer in Faxe Ladeplads. The town population quadruples because of all the people from Copenhagen who own summer cottages out here in the country, as they call it. The city buzzes with life, and there's a disco every weekend at the hotel and at Gefion. The girls from school are allowed to leave the premises, as long as we promise to watch out for each other and come home together.

We dance from when we arrive until we head home at five in the morning. The first night, there's a group of really well-dressed guys, who the other girls tell me are from Herlufsholm, a private boarding school. Their parents own either a house or a cottage in Faxe Ladeplads, and they're famous for drinking themselves silly and chasing the local girls.

I think they look hot. They're all wearing polo shirts—Kappa or Lacoste—with small neckerchiefs inside the collar, and torn jeans. I want to rip my jeans the same way; Kirsten should be able to help me with that. And they dance really well. They stand around in a circle dancing with each other, occasionally checking out the other partygoers. A bunch of snobs, say the others.

But I like them, especially one tall, thin, blond guy whose name is Klaus. He dances by me at one point, grabs my arms, and swings me around, all the while screaming along with David Bowie's "China Girl." We dance to a few songs without speaking, and then he asks if I want to get some fresh air.

"Yes," I say, thinking I'll stay close to the entrance. I'm not going to make that mistake again.

We walk out into the warm summer night. Now he's singing along to some song about a "summer girl" while twirling me around. At one point, we spin and fall laughing on the sidewalk. We just lie there, our legs and bodies out in the street, with the curb as our pillow, talking about the stars and our parents. He tells me his parents are diplomats who work abroad; that's why he's living at Herlufsholm. Laughing, we agree that we're both living in orphanages—except his is the one for the rich kids. Klaus isn't snobby at all. He's just giddy and has a cheerful attitude about life. And we make each other laugh until we cry.

When the club closes, he asks if I'll be there tomorrow. Maybe, I say. Then he starts singing again about his "summer girl," skipping home on the road by the shore. I head in the opposite direction with the other girls from school.

I can't wait until tomorrow evening. A large group of girls goes with us this time. I've spent hours putting on my makeup, which I rarely do. I have on my new blouse with the dolman sleeves, along with a pair of jeans I've torn to shreds at the knees and in the backside, so you can see the bottom of my cheeks and a bit of my panties. Klaus isn't there when we arrive. In fact, several hours pass before he and the other guys from Herlufsholm show up. By that time, I've given up on him and have my eye on the DJ. And he's had his eye on me.

Without my noticing it, Klaus has danced his way over until he's close enough to swing me around, which makes me dizzy. He's laughing, reeks of liquor, and is barely standing up—but I don't care. We dance to a couple of songs before he asks if I want to go outside.

Once again, we walk out into the warm summer night; unlike the last time, Klaus starts kissing me, again and again, and telling me how sexy I look in my jeans. He can't concentrate when he's looking at me. After a little while, he asks if I want to go home with him.

High on the feeling that I'm sexy, I say yes. I don't say a word to the other girls. Wrapped around each other, we walk to his house and go down into the basement, which is like a separate apartment. He says it's all his. We head straight for the bed, where we tear each other's clothes off. He doesn't waste any time trying to make me feel safe and warm—he just penetrates me. For a moment, I feel frightened, but I go through with the intercourse anyway.

Afterward, Klaus falls right to sleep, but I lie there looking around. I'm so cold that my teeth are chattering, so I get up, put on my clothes, and walk back to the club to be with the others. I don't say anything; I just sit down on the plush sofa and watch the others dancing. Suddenly the DJ announces that the next song is dedicated to the naughty little girl sitting alone on the sofa. I look up at him and he winks back at me. I smile wryly and stare a little too long into his eyes as Nanna's "Buster" echoes across the dance floor.

That night with Klaus is just the start of a marathon of one-night stands. I don't know why, but whenever I can seize the chance to turn some guy on, I go all the way. It doesn't matter if it's the back seat of a car, on a playground, or behind some tanks where soldiers are doing drills. Having sex doesn't hurt anymore, and I'm not afraid. For a brief moment, I'm the world's most important person for the man who has me—and I've discovered that I can have anyone I want. All I have to do is dress provocatively and stare intensely without averting my gaze when they look back. When I'm at a club, before I go home, I'll target someone who wants me, and it usually works.

Niels is fading more and more from my consciousness. One day I write him a letter and end it all. I'm sad for him, but I'm feeling a rush of power over the men who drive off with me—and there's no room for Niels.

Rigmor knows what I'm up to. None of it is affecting my performance as a student at Hylleholt, yet I'm well aware of her disappointed stares and tart comments that I should cover myself up more.

I continue exploring my newfound abilities during summer vacation in Nakskov. I spend the first week at the Palshøjs'. I have to go on a camping trip with them: five of us in a Combi-Camp tent trailer. The Palshøjs are sweet people, but that week I feel like a lion in a cage. I wander around smoking like a fiend and searching for new victims. Unfortunately, all I can find at the campgrounds are small, irritating boys and overweight dads.

I spend the next week with Mom. My plan is to lure her into a disco with me. I'm determined to explore Nakskov seriously—and Mom's along for the ride. We hit both El Paso and Bristol, the two clubs in town. Entrance is free at El Paso, the shabbier bar. Bristol, the nicer of the two, has a plush red interior with tons of blinking lights and disco balls. We go back and forth between the two clubs, while I search for suitable victims. The DJ at El Paso fits the bill: his name is Teddy, and before long I've established contact. I wind up going home with him the next morning. Before that, Mom and I dance to all the songs we can handle—she's happy, proudly telling anyone who will listen that she's in the city with her daughter. I don't care. She's just a pretext.

Teddy, who's twenty-one, lives alone in a studio apartment. I spend the rest of my vacation waiting for Teddy at El Paso and then going home with him. We only get together at night.

After summer vacation, when I'm starting ninth grade, Karen, the social worker who's married to Børge, returns to Hylleholt. Karen has dark, curly hair and intense, wise, deep-set eyes. She's slender and beautiful in a classical way. A little like Karen Blixen, the dark edition. At this time, I've been working my way through Blixen's oeuvre, and that's one of the first two things we discuss: Karen Blixen and books.

My first day back, while we're having coffee on the patio, we discover our shared sense of humor. I've never met anyone who enjoys what I have to say so much—and I'm sold! I love Karen and think she has it all. She has Børge, and she's beautiful and smart and funny. That's how I want to be.

The days are all a little happier and deeper when Karen's at work. I try to spend as much time with her as possible, and I'm thrilled when they decide Karen's going to help me with German. After summer vacation, I stopped taking extra classes with Kubel, but I still need help: Karen is the only one at Hylleholt with a high school diploma.

As we work on my German and discuss literature together, something resembling a friendship emerges between us. Like Rigmor, Karen loans me books, and I soon become acquainted with Fay Weldon, Marge Piercy, and Erica Jong—authors who represent a world I know nothing about. All of their books deal with intelligent women repressed by men and the society around them. Women who discover alternative ways of living; women who avenge themselves. I really like that last part.

That fall, a new girl named Bettina moves into Hylleholt. She's short, compact, and blonde, and she has strong, beautiful features. I'm drawn to her aggressiveness. There's no bullshit about her—she says exactly what she means. Whereas I'm always looking for an escape route before I attack someone, Bettina goes straight for the jugular. She's the first student at Hylleholt I share a true friendship with. Bettina's also from Nakskov, and we're inseparable from the first weekend we go back home together.

Karen Gjesing photographed at home. Karen was the one social worker who was able to help me open up about the sexual assaults. Over the years, I've remained close with both Karen and her ex-husband, Børge.

Bettina and I go into town every night we can. Sometimes Mom comes along: she really wants to, and she loves to dance. For the first time in my childhood, I feel as if we're starting to have a relationship. She beams while wriggling around the dance floor, and men, both young and old, take notice. She looks right into their eyes and smiles as she gyrates her hips. Mom's thirty-seven at this point and still attractive.

Now and then, Richard hears about her provocative dancing and knocks her around. It doesn't scare her, though. Thank God I'm witnessing these beatings less and less frequently. Often, I've either gone home with some guy or I'm sleeping over at Bettina's parents' house. When I do go out with Mom—and we come home in the wee hours of the morning—Richard's usually fast asleep in his chair. We sneak into bed, knowing she's going to get it the next day. By that time, however, I've gone for a walk or am off visiting someone. I always wake up first: whenever we've been in town, I'm restless and unable to sleep for long. That way, I'm able to slip out and avoid Richard's violence and Mom's pleas.

Before long, it's spring, and I've been living at Hylleholt for a whole year. I celebrate my fifteenth birthday there, and my gift is a briefcase. Other than the bike I got from Mom and Richard, I've never been so happy about a gift. Now I have to decide what I'm going to do after summer vacation. I have no doubts—I want to go to high school, and Rigmor, Karen, and Britt agree. If I continue my schooling, I'll be the first student from Hylleholt to get a high school diploma, which means a great deal to all of them. They're as proud as parents.

I decide to pursue the linguistic track. The only other student from my class going to high school is Fatina, but we choose different schools. I want to go to Haslev, which seems like an academically sound school, whereas Fatina wants to go to Køge, which is known for being more creative.

Soon it's time for our final exams. I'm nervous about German, so I study for it as much as I can in my packed schedule. Declensions are rolling around inside my head, and Karen diligently reviews everything with me.

Exam day finally arrives. I'm the last one to take the oral exam. There have been a couple of A-minuses; otherwise all the grades so far have been between a C and a B. Kubel's students always do well. Now it's my turn, and I choose a text I can read aloud and discuss. While I'm preparing, my heart is beating so hard I'm having trouble breathing; as I walk up to the desk, my ears are ringing so loudly I can barely hear what Kubel and the examiner are saying. It all occurs in a fog, and as I leave the room, I have no idea how it went.

A short time passes, and then the door opens and Kubel comes out, a big smile on his face.

"How do you think you did, Lisbeth?" he asks.

"I don't know," I say as my ears start ringing again.

"A-minus. Congratulations!" He gives me a wink.

All I can do is smile. If I open my mouth to say anything, I'll start crying and I don't want to. He turns to go back in the exam room.

The mood back at Hylleholt is festive. Karen gives me a big hug, and the other adults congratulate me. It's a big day. I wasn't nervous about the other subjects, but I was really worried about German.

Summer vacation rolls around again, and I'm off to Nakskov. This time, Fatina comes with me. We're going to spend a week with Mom and then two weeks with the Palshøjs. I introduce Fatina to the club scene in Nakskov on the very first day. El Paso is open every night, and we're loyal customers: we're there from when the music starts until closing time. One night, I meet a blond guy named Ib who's twenty-three and has his own apartment. He's a sergeant at Vordingborg Barracks. Meanwhile Fatina meets Henrik, and we soon fall into a pattern of dividing our time between the two guys and each other. The first week goes by in a flash. Sometimes Mom comes along, and we're partying almost all day long.

The following week we're at the Palshøjs', where we continue pursuing our nightlife. They insist that we be home by eleven each night, but we totally ignore them. We come home when we want to—if we come home at all. After one week, they demand that we go back to Faxe Ladeplads. Birthe says they can no longer be responsible for us.

I arrive at Hylleholt a week early with a letter from the Palshøjs for Rigmor, which I'm not allowed to open. I hand it to her as soon as I arrive, and after reading it, Rigmor looks up at me.

"You don't want to stay with them anymore, do you?" she asks.

"No," I reply. "As I've said many times."

"Okay. Then that's how it will be."

1983–84

On August 8, 1983, I start high school in Haslev. I'm the youngest in my class, which consists of six boys and twice as many girls. I have no idea what it's like to go to high school. The only person I know who's been is Karen—and that was twenty years ago. But I soon realize that high school is a lot like grade school: classroom instruction with a few more subjects, including Latin. Latin is a logical language when it comes to writing; it reminds me of German with its strict grammar rules. It seems only natural that Karen and I continue our studies together—only now we focus on Latin and French. I really value our sessions, which deal mostly with academics but sometimes expand into talking about being young in general. Still, though, we never discuss my personal problems. I've already rejected therapy sessions once, clearly signaling that if they leave my mental state alone, I'll function just fine.

I feel right at home in high school. My teachers are knowledgeable and dedicated to their subjects. I throw myself into all of it—especially social studies. I buy a cap with the Red Army star on it, just like Karen's husband, Børge, and some mandarin-collar shirts. I also start smoking King's cigarettes, which feel more intellectual than Princes, and throw myself into poetry: Suzanne Brøgger, Lola Baidel, Dan Turèll, Holger Drachmann, and Thorkild Bjørnvig. I start writing more of my own poems too. In Danish, I usually turn in poems or analyze them when I get the chance—and I even flirt with the idea of becoming a writer.

At some point, I write a short romance story, which I send to a women's magazine. Inspired by Mom and Richard's relationship, it describes one of the times Richard knocked her around. I want to write about a love that's difficult. It's rejected, which compels me to abandon my dream of becoming an author.

Afterward, I turn my attention to socially relevant subjects. In class I argue a lot—and loudly. Soon I'm known as that irritating social critic you need stamina to keep up with. Eventually I gain enough confidence to tease my teachers, who tease me right back, which is a great joy.

One day I keep interrupting my French teacher because I disagree with her interpretation of *Le Boucher*. Finally she walks over, grabs my hair, and places my head, facedown, on my desk; meanwhile, she continues speaking calmly in French. She stands there for a good five minutes before she lets go and then walks back up to her desk. Next French class, I show up in a crew cut, proclaiming in my broken French that she can't shut me up like that anymore just because we don't agree. We have a good laugh over it.

My geography teacher, whom we call Geo-Svend, regularly throws an eraser to make me stop talking. High school represents a new and fantastic world for me, and I get along with the other students too. Especially Helle, who's a good head taller than me and has long, blonde, permed hair and sea-blue eyes surrounded by the longest eyelashes I've ever seen. She's smart and beautiful—but she talks like a truck driver, so I chuckle every time she opens her mouth. She's also the first in her family to go to high school. We start to hang out during our free periods, whenever we have the time. Haslev is a good distance from Faxe Ladeplads, so I have to take a bus to school and back, on top of my tight schedule of cleaning, food prep, and rowing at Hylleholt. Not to mention Fatina, whom I want to keep seeing. Helle goes to dance class several times a week and works at a kiosk, but we see each other after school as often as we can.

I continue to pursue my active weekends in Nakskov. I usually go into town with Bettina, and when she can't, I take Mom. I don't tell my classmates what I'm doing on the weekends—only that I'm going home to see my mother, who lives far away, and that I live in a kind of boarding school. The feeling of living a double life has never been stronger, but for me it works just fine.

There are some high school parties, but I inform Hylleholt that I have no intention of going to any of the school's dances. Rigmor and Karen gang up on me, though, and insist that I go. Karen even drives me to one, but as soon as she drives away, I walk down to the bus stop and take the bus back to Faxe Ladeplads. They don't get to decide whether or not I'm going to dances at the high school—I can't imagine anything worse. To me, beer, dancing, and music mean Nakskov—I don't see any reason to involve my school in any of that.

Soon it becomes a bone of contention between Rigmor and me. She thinks I don't have any friends in my class and don't want boyfriends my own age. But that's not it. I like my classmates, and the feeling is mutual. I can't explain why the parties are such a problem.

In December of 1983, Rigmor asks me to spend Christmas with her in Thy. That autumn she knitted a sweater for me, and she often takes me with her to different places, like Copenhagen when she wants to shop. Sometimes she invites me to an elegant dinner at her apartment, where the table is set with Royal Copenhagen porcelain and crystal glasses. Once she even asks me to spend the night in her apartment so I can answer the phone while she goes out to find a student who's run away. Clearly, my status is special—she has high expectations of me. It makes me happy, yet at the same time it frustrates me that I have to be ashamed of seeking out the environment I come from.

Although I say yes to spending Christmas with her and her family, I don't really want to. Still, I don't want to appear ungrateful by saying no. The holiday soon approaches, and two days before Christmas Eve, I knock on her office door. She's sitting at her desk writing something. I tell her I've decided not to go home with her. She doesn't look up.

"Okay. What have you decided to do?" she asks, still writing.

"Go home to be with my mother," I say.

"All right, then," Rigmor says, still not looking up.

The conversation is obviously over, so I leave. I don't know why I don't want to go with her; I just don't, even if it disappoints her.

That Christmas, Richard beats Mom so badly that he smashes her dentures and her eyes are swollen shut. When it starts, I grab my jacket and leave. I'm done with their fighting. But I don't get far before I can't take the thought of Mom being hurt and not being there to help her.

When I get back, they're still going at it. Richard is punching her in the stomach and face. She's next to the coffee table, so she grabs a thermos and slams it into the back of Richard's head. You can hear the glass shatter inside it. As he lets go of her to grab his head, she runs into the bathroom. Moaning, Richard sits down in a leather chair. A little while later she comes out and announces that she's taken a whole bottle of sleeping pills.

"It's about fucking time!" says Richard as he grabs his jacket and leaves.

Mom runs screaming around the living room for a while until she finally lies down in the fetal position on the sofa. Did she really take all those pills?

"You don't even take sleeping pills," I say, "so why in the world would you suddenly have a whole bottle of them?"

She doesn't respond.

"I think I'm going to just fucking leave. That way you can die in peace," I say, standing up.

She struggles up on one elbow.

"Don't leave me, Lisbeth. You're all I have left. No one likes me. Not even you. I'd be better off dead," she says, sniffling.

I don't say anything. Can't. My jaw is clenched—and if I open it, all that's going to come out is rage. I call for an ambulance. It's the middle of the night by the time she's lying in a hospital bed and sleeping, her shattered dentures sitting in a glass next to her. Out in the hall, a nurse stops me and asks where I'm going.

"Don't worry about it," I tell her as I leave to see Henrik, the DJ at Bristol.

Back at Hylleholt, Rigmor seems distant. I get it. I was ungrateful about Christmas, and now, on top of everything else, I've come back announcing what a shitty Christmas it's been.

After that last attack, the hospital reports Richard to the police, and I'm called as a witness in the court case in Nakskov. I have to appear in court one morning in March. I've just turned sixteen. Both Mom and Richard are sitting there; neither of them looks at me. I'm asked to describe in detail what I saw, and I do so exactly as I remember it—including the episode with the coffee thermos. Along the way I try to make eye contact with Mom, but she stares down at the table the entire time. I'm there for ten minutes at the most before I'm asked to leave the courtroom. Out in the hall, a sweet bailiff tells me I can be reimbursed for the time I've had to spend in court, and I'm given some money. Then I go back home.

The next time I'm in Nakskov, I find out that all charges have been dropped. In court Mom said I lied—that Richard was only defending himself against her attack, and that's why she was so banged up. There was a big article in *New Day*, where they made fools of both her and me. I race back to her apartment, where she's watching TV.

"Why the fuck did you say I lied in court?" I scream at her.

Terrified, she stares at me: normally I don't yell at her.

"I didn't dare do anything else, Mouse," she says in her little-girl voice.

I storm out the door.

From that day on, I start to have nightmares about beating the hell out of her. I'm trying to strangle her while slamming the back of her head into a wall. Kicking her, over and over again, in the stomach, until blood flows out of her mouth. I wake up almost every night bathed in sweat. I'm becoming increasingly afraid to go to bed. It's like a war is raging inside my head every night, and I can't make it stop. I try counting, like in the old days, but it doesn't work anymore. I don't tell anyone about it. I don't know why, but the dreams are so violent that I'm afraid of being viewed as sick if I tell anyone about them.

Rigmor starts riding me because I'm always reading or doing homework when I have free time at Hylleholt. She says I must think I'd die if I had to do manual labor. I can use my hands—I already proved that in metal shop—and I always do my daily chores. But I'd rather write an essay or recite classical works than stand there in the kitchen.

She suggests I get a part-time job, so I can learn to use my hands and understand what it means to earn money. "Okay," I say. I'd rather not discuss what's best with her. Mental or physical labor. A few days later she tells me she's found me a job with the local butcher, Svendsen. I'll be working as a dishwasher and cleaning assistant on Saturdays.

Inge-Lise and Henning Svendsen own a large butcher shop in the center of Faxe Ladeplads. It reeks of smoked meat and wood—the latter because of all the fresh sawdust Svendsen strews on the floor after it's been cleaned. The atmosphere in the shop is really pleasant; journey-men and assistants work effectively, all the while chatting and laughing.

Grethe, who makes the open-faced sandwiches, calls me "little Lisbeth" and gives me a big hug every chance she gets. I just love her. Inge-Lise is as sweet as Grethe, and when she has time, she teaches me everything from taking care of the cheese case to making sandwiches.

Henning—or just Svendsen, as we call him—is a short, strong man who wears a red-and-white apron and a black derby. Even though he doesn't talk as much as the women, I can tell he likes me. Before long, he's teaching me everything about how to carve beef, grind meat, vacuum pack, make pork crackling, and pump up the pork saddle. Also how to use the cash register and deal with the customers. I really like the latter, and a few months after I'm hired, I'm allowed to serve customers and carve beef out of expensive pieces of meat, like fillet and tenderloin.

I love my job there. Every Saturday before the first of the month, once I've cleaned the floor and scoured the cheese case, I'm handed a brown envelope with my pay. I hand the envelope over to Hylleholt, where they keep it for me so I can save up for bigger things.

Sometimes Rigmor shows up to buy meat, and I get to wait on her. I'm not sure who's prouder—her or me.

My life is busy. I'm rowing, running, sewing clothes, going to school, doing my homework, seeing friends, taking care of my chores at Hylleholt, working at Svendsen's several days a week now, and doing the bar scene in Nakskov every other weekend.

I'm so busy that any change to my daily schedule makes me feel as if I'm going to have a breakdown. I want to smash everything around me, although I don't do it. Everything goes dark, and I see red until I can't even think straight. It might be a bus to Haslev that's late, a canceled class at school, or Hylleholt wanting me to participate in something without warning me ahead of time.

One day Karen asks if we should expand our study session to include personal issues. My immediate impulse is to say no, but I trust

Karen, who's now been named my guardian. I sense that I need to do something about all my rage, which I never show anyone, although it's eating me up inside.

We start with a weekly discussion that takes place in a different room from where we do homework. "So we're not mixing up homework and personal matters," says Karen.

Karen lets me talk about whatever comes to mind. She doesn't offer any answers; she just asks questions. Sometimes we sit in silence while I'm either thinking or struggling to hold back the tears. She doesn't force me to say anything. She just listens and asks questions and is silent until I answer. Yet, I still can't talk about the violence and the sexual assaults—or about the change in my personality when I'm in Nakskov, which makes me ashamed.

We talk a lot about shame, actually, and she says that nothing children like me have experienced is shameful. If anyone should feel shame, it's the adults who've let it happen. I hear what she's saying but I don't agree. I'm afraid that people will look at me in a different or negative way if they know what I've experienced and how I behaved. Karen, especially, mustn't see me that way.

We continue our conversations through the next few months. They don't make me uncomfortable, but I become increasingly frustrated that I can't get any further—that I'm unable to talk about what really matters. I say that to Karen. After summer vacation, in September of 1984, Karen brings a video camera to one of our conversations.

"What do you say we film you, Lisbeth, and then watch the tape together?" she asks.

I don't know what good that will do.

"It might be good for you to experience yourself," she says. "Maybe you can see the fine person the rest of us see when we look at you. Even when we aren't looking at your grades or your ability to slice exactly seven ounces of roast beef."

"Okay."

Karen turns on the videocam. I move around the room and respond to what she's asking me. She asks me to sing a song. I sing a couple of songs I remember the lyrics to, and then she turns off the camera. She puts the videotape in a player and we watch it together. I think my voice sounds hoarse. And I'm way too thin and round shouldered. And my cheeks are too fat. I tell all that to Karen.

"Know what I see, Lisbeth? I see a young girl who's carrying too much weight on her shoulders," she says.

I can't hold back the tears any longer. I cry as I try to tell her about Jan and Mom's assaults on me in Torrig. I could tell her about so many other terrible experiences, but that's the one I land on. I describe in detail what happened, what was said at the time, how often it happened, and that they were both there, although Mom clearly didn't want to be. She just couldn't refuse; she couldn't protect me. I tell her about Mom saying Jan should make sure no one could tell. I felt as if my words would mean nothing—only physical evidence would. I sob, my head against her shoulder. I can't see Karen's face and I don't want to; I don't want her to be frightened. She holds me until my sobbing turns into sniffling and I'm overcome with exhaustion. Something I almost never feel.

"I'm proud of you, Lisbeth. Now we'll pack up our equipment—and I think you should blow your nose and wash your face. We'll continue this discussion next week, if you want to."

"Thanks," I say and then go to my room, where I lie down on my bed and fall asleep.

I'm awakened by the bell that always rings when it's mealtime at Hylleholt. I'm light-headed. In the dining hall, I sit there, my eyes red and my face swollen, and laugh at everything. I feel like I've been drinking. I look over at Karen, who's sitting at another table. She looks the same as always, which I don't understand; it's as if she hears the kinds of things I've told her every day. But maybe she does. Maybe some of the other girls have had the same experiences—we just don't share them with each other or the other adults.

That same week, I decide I'm never going to Nakskov again. Rigmor informs Mom, though I have no idea how she responds or if they even tell her the reason. Hylleholt notifies Ravnsborg township about the assaults, but no police report is filed. I don't ask why, and Mom doesn't try to contact me.

Karen and I continue our weekly discussions, which I really look forward to: we leave no stone unturned. We talk a lot about my time at the orphanage in Nakskov, especially the loneliness I felt and my inability to say what was wrong. All I could do was act up and feel bad about it. Instead of trying to find out why I was misbehaving, they simply told me to change my behavior and not take advantage of Mom, who was having a hard time.

I also tell Karen about my counting obsession, which she finds amusing; she says it's completely normal for children who feel unsafe to use rituals to bring stability to their lives. And here I thought I was just crazy.

When I don't spend the weekend at Hylleholt, I go home with Karen and Børge, who live close to Faxe. As if by magic, the urge to go out and get laid has vanished. I work as much as I can at Svendsen's, do my schoolwork, and see my friends. I spend the weekends with Karen and Børge on the big couch in their living room, where there's also a large bookcase full of books and comics. I read from morning till night, stopping only to sleep.

I'm tired in a way I've never known, so I have to sleep several times a day. I like it best when I fall asleep to the sound of Karen's and Børge's voices. I'm incredibly tired in school too, and they have to wake me up in German, Danish, English, and French. It can't go on—but I'll find some solution. During lunch, I go down to the girls' locker room and lie on a bench, my arms folded behind my head. If I sleep for ten minutes, I can stay awake until I'm on the bus to Faxe Ladeplads, where I can catch another half hour of sleep.

A few months after my conversation with Karen, Rigmor suggests that I start thinking about leaving Hylleholt. It's just before Christmas of 1984, and I'm shocked the first time she says it. I'm sixteen, in my junior year, and have broken all ties with my family. I have a couple of friends my own age and a boyfriend named Teddy who's more like a friend than a lover. Otherwise all I have in life are the butcher shop and the social workers at Hylleholt. I feel betrayed. Is this the thanks I get for opening up? I know girls can remain at Hylleholt until they're eighteen, so why can't I? And where am I supposed to live?

A typical shot of me at Hylleholt: no concern for my looks and lost in a book.

Rigmor says there's not much more they can do for me—I need to get out of the cocoon I've created for myself. Karen, who supports Rigmor's decision, says they've found a psychologist named Mei-Mei in Copenhagen who specializes in my kind of trauma and that Ravnsborg township will pay for it.

Karen will still be my guardian, so I'll always have one, at least until I'm eighteen. I don't understand. I feel broken and frightened. But they're firm in their decision: come April, I'll move to student housing at a teachers college close to my high school in Haslev. I keep protesting, though I know it won't do any good. I need to prepare myself for leaving Faxe Ladeplads and the sanctuary of the rowing club, Svendsen's, Fatina, and Hylleholt.

Karen and I start to figure out how much money I'll be seeking from the township for furnishing my room—and what I can pay out of my savings from my job at Svendsen's. I keep working there, but I decide to drop rowing.

I spend the Christmas before I move with Karen and Børge. Their Christmas tree is huge and the food is scrumptious. Both Karen and Børge have bought me gifts—books—and Hylleholt has given me a book also. No gifts from Mom or Dad. A few days later, I get a package from Mom: a summer dress from a discount store with the sales tag still on it. The dress doesn't fit. And there's no card.

Naturally, Karen and Børge's children, Anders and Bolette, are also home for Christmas. Bolette is two years younger than me, and Anders is three years younger. Anders is a mini-version of Karen, whereas Bolette looks more like her father. Whenever I spend the night there, I sleep on a mattress in Bolette's room. I could easily sleep in a separate room, but Bolette and I hit it off from the moment we meet. I'm the older one who smokes and tells horrible stories about a reality she'll never know, and she's the creative and imaginative one who draws comics I can barely understand. Anders is the world's happiest kid, but I think Bolette is too hard on him.

Every night they have to clean up after dinner—and every night they fight like cats and dogs about who's washing and who's drying. I try to mediate the nightly feuds, so we can all enjoy ourselves (although Bolette thinks I'm too soft on Anders).

Bolette and I are listening to some adults talking at the home of her parents, Karen and Børge. At this time, I was going to high school dressed in very masculine clothes, with no makeup or jewelry. I recognize that expression on my face. I don't recall why I have it here, but it illustrates my ability to leave my body and my surroundings and disappear. I continue to wrestle with this response mechanism when I find myself in conflict situations. I still see Bolette and her brother, Anders, and consider them part of my family.

Karen and Børge take me on vacation to a farm out in the country in Sweden. Bolette and I also go to Copenhagen by ourselves several times; we hit the used bookstores and Fantask to buy some comics. Both Karen and Børge say that I have to keep visiting them—that they'll miss me if I stop coming. It makes me feel safe.

Two months before I leave to go live in college housing, I turn seventeen. Hylleholt bakes me a cake, and once again I get a book as a gift. I get one from Karen and Børge too, but the fact that Mom forgets my birthday depresses me.

"Who will remember my birthday once I leave here?" I ask Karen and Rigmor, my eyes filled with furious tears.

"I will," replies Karen. But I'm not convinced.

Afternoon tea with Karen and Børge. I'm sitting with Bolette and Karen on their gigantic couch, my favorite spot in the house. I could easily spend a whole day there reading their books and comics— barely visible behind us—interrupted only by brief naps. I started sleeping quite a bit after I opened up about my sexual abuse during therapy sessions. I used to love falling asleep at Karen and Børge's while listening to their conversations.

I pack mechanically and absentmindedly. Once I've filled Karen's car with my things, I walk around to say goodbye. Both students and adults get hugs, and the tears flow. I've stopped trying to hold them back. The last person I say goodbye to is Rigmor, who gives me a long hug. Then she smiles broadly and, in her thick Jutland accent, says: "Keep up the good fight, Lisbeth."

I'm still mad at her, but I'm going to miss her. She's been hard on me—sometimes unreasonably hard—but she does care about me. And she's really only been unreasonable when I've disappointed her. In a way, it's nice that she cares so much about me that I can disappoint her.

"See you at my graduation party," I say and walk out the door.

I wonder if I'll ever see Hylleholt again.

1984–86

Kære Rigmor.   Haslev d. 6.4.-85.

Ja, nu er jeg altså voksen. Kan bruge min frihed til, hvad jeg vil. Kan gå i seng, når jeg har lyst. Jeg kan faktisk alt, hvad jeg har lyst til. Det er også meget godt. Ja, for jeg har da udnyttet min frihed. Jeg har da været i Næstved, hvor jeg var på restaurant med Teddy og bagefter i biografen. Om natten sov jeg hos ham. Se, det var min frihed, jeg dér udnyttede. Men ved du hvad, Rigmor? HOLD KÆFT, HVOR ER DET TRIST at være voksen. Dermed ikke sagt, at jeg fortryder. Det gør jeg bestemt ikke. Jeg skal bare lære ikke at have travlt. Bare tage det stille og roligt, så at min tid bliver disponeret fornuftigt og ikke rase afsted. Lige nu virker alt bare så uoverskueligt. Jeg synes, alle mine muligheder hvirvler omkring hovedet på mig så stærkt, at det er umuligt for mig at gribe dem. Det eneste fornuftige, jeg har foretaget, er dette brev her. Ellers har jeg bare cyklet lidt omkring og hørt Erik Grip. Han er den eneste, der kan få mig til at falde lidt til ro og tænke rationelt.
Jeg har forøvrigt overvejet, om det ikke var en fejl at flytte i en ferie? Hvis det var i skole-tiden, ville jeg ikke have haft tid til at

I was deeply lonely when I wrote Rigmor this letter, dated April 6, 1985. In it, I tell her that I can do whatever I want with my newfound freedom—but that I find being an adult sad. I admit that I have to learn how to be less busy. I tell her that everything seems confusing and I'm overwhelmed by possibilities. I also question whether it might have been better to have moved during the school year

tænke på min "umulige" situation og blive
rigtig ~~selvoptaget~~ selvoptaget.
Jeg indrømmer, jeg savner min skole !!! Jeg
glæder mig ikke til, jeg er færdiguddannet.

Kærlig hilsen

Lisbeth Andersen.

PS: Hvis du en dag har overskud til en
gammel elev så send en kærlig hilsen
til mig!

rather than over vacation, as I've now had too much time to think about my "impossible situation."
Finally I admit to missing Hylleholt; I'm not looking forward to finishing my education. In my PS, I
ask Rigmor to write to this "old student" if she has any extra time.

I've been living on my own for seven days now. I'm seventeen years and two months old and about to become an adult. I make my own food, wash my own clothes, clean, do my homework, pay the bills, juggle school and sleep, and take care of whatever else is needed to be an adult. None of it scares me. I've signed a renter's policy with Codan Insurance. I'm totally on top of that kind of stuff.

The loneliness terrifies me, however. I bike all over Haslev and the surrounding area, with no idea what to do with myself. Out to Bregentved Manor and then to Gisselfeld Castle, where I take long walks through the garden and greenhouses. By Easter I've logged quite a few miles—but I don't ride back to Faxe Ladeplads. It's not my town anymore; I only go there when I have to work at Svendsen's.

When I'm not out riding my bike, I'm lying on my bed reading. I have stacks of library books, which I devour greedily. Tom Kristensen's dark novel *Havoc* has a profound effect on me, though it doesn't do much for my mood, and Günter Grass's *The Tin Drum*, about a boy who doesn't want to grow up, makes me even more depressed.

I don't have a television and have no desire to hang out in the kitchen with the others, who are all at least three years older. They're attending a teachers college—and I haven't even finished junior year of high school. If only it weren't Easter vacation. Now and then I see Marianne and Helle from my class, and I've visited Teddy a few times also. But I really miss adults giving me a hug good night and eating breakfast with me. I can always call Karen, but it's not the same—and I don't want to be running to her and Børge every five minutes.

So, I write a letter to Rigmor and hope she'll respond or maybe even come to visit. I miss her and Hylleholt terribly, but I'm also angry. I still don't understand why I couldn't just stay there. I'm not ready to live on my own. Nobody else from my class is living on their own—so why do I have to? Why was Rigmor in such a hurry? What did I ever do to her? That's what bothers me most of all. What did I ever do to her?

For two and a half tranquil years, I was able to live in peace at Hylleholt. The minute I tell someone about being sexually assaulted, and all those other disgusting experiences, I'm dismissed. Why is it better for me to live alone in this cubbyhole, with a weekly visit to a psychologist in Copenhagen, than to stay at Hylleholt and have weekly conversations with Karen? I'm just so incredibly sad about it.

After spending a whole day by myself, where the only voice I hear is my own, it all seems senseless. I feel like the loneliest person in the world as I eat dinner—some frozen rice dish I thawed out in the sink and then mixed with a can of tuna. I eat sitting on my bed, a book in one hand. My friends aren't going to call to say good night. They have no idea what it's like to sit all alone staring at four walls.

The sleep problems I'd finally gotten a handle on at Hylleholt start to flare up again. First I spend hours trying to fall asleep, and then I wake up repeatedly, bathed in sweat, because of the nightmares I keep having. Most of them are about Mom. And the day starts at six a.m., whether or not I have anything to do.

Easter vacation ends, and I finally start school again. My classmates can't believe I'm living alone.

"That's so cool," they tell me.

"It's okay," I say. "You decide when to eat and when to go to bed."

All through Easter vacation I've been living off the same combo of frozen rice and tuna, except at breakfast when I've been eating crisp-bread with creamy Havarti. I'm a good cook—but what's the point of making Salisbury steak for one?

I have enough money. Karen and Hylleholt have seen to it that I receive the cash equivalent of benefits. Even though I'm not eighteen yet, it's not a problem. Ravnsborg township has already agreed to pay benefits when I turn eighteen. The others from my class receive only student grants, whereas I get a couple of thousand extra kroner to spend on food, clothes, and books. And nights out.

I've started going to Black and White, a disco here in Haslev, with Helle. We call it B & W. Less than a year ago, I was in a bar every night I spent in Nakskov. I always found someone to have sex with, in a courtyard behind the bar or at the guy's place—it didn't matter. Helle doesn't know anything about that, and I'm a different person now, anyway. But how does this new Lisbeth spend a night in town without coming on to someone?

Turns out it's not a problem. Helle goes into town to dance, so we dance our way through the weekends. Only rarely do we let guys disturb our routine. Helle, who's taken lessons for years, is a dream to watch on the dance floor. I keep up as best I can. She can swing me around and keep us moving in a way that makes me feel high. We rarely drink alcohol—and we never go home with any guys.

Now and then I see Teddy. Sometimes we have sex, but we're mostly just friends. Crazy friends who chase each other all over Faxe and who slip Tabasco sauce into his mother's breakfast. I feel as if I've known him forever. I happily take part in his escapades, whether he needs my body or my sense of craziness.

My friends start to take up more of my time. Fatina and I are still in touch, but she dropped out of high school and moved to London to dance. I still have Helle and Marianne, though. Marianne is back for her junior year: she spent a year as an exchange student in the United States, has a driver's license, a car, and a horse. Her father is a successful artist, and her mother is an elegant woman who drives a big car into Copenhagen every week to play bridge. Marianne has two rooms at her parents' place: a dressing room and a bedroom.

They live in a huge, renovated farmhouse with large rooms and a gigantic kitchen. Her mother is rarely home, and her father is always in his studio, so we usually have the house to ourselves. We spend hours watching Monty Python on the large-screen TV in one of their living rooms. Marianne can make me cry with laughter in no time. In music class, for example, the teacher asks if any of us can play a musical instrument, and without missing a beat, Marianne says that she plays the skin flute. I spend the rest of the class laughing. Marianne is a comedian who keeps my spirits up, and Helle is a dancing fairy who makes my weekends fly by.

I work every Friday afternoon and Saturday morning at Svendsen's, and now and then I sleep at their house instead of taking the bus back and forth. Once I've moved, it feels strange coming back to Faxe Ladeplads. Every time I step off the bus, I look around for Rigmor and the students. Sometimes I see some of them, but I don't make my presence known. Hylleholt isn't my home anymore—but I still get a feeling in the pit of my stomach whenever I meet anyone I know from there.

Sometimes Rigmor stops in at Svendsen's to buy meat. She always waits until I have time to take care of her. I get so nervous when she's in the shop.

"How's it going, Lisbeth?" she asks in her familiar accent.

"Fine."

I fill her order, all the while thinking that other students will be eating it. Not me. Anger and sorrow rage within me as I ring her up, my heart pounding.

I'm starting to get used to living as an outcast in Haslev. During the week, only the late-evening hours are hard, because they remind me that I'm alone. When visiting Karen and Børge, I get a lot of attention. I enjoy all the physical contact and our conversations about everything under the sun, but none of that does me any good during the week. At the butcher shop, Grethe and Inge-Lise shower me with big, warm hugs, but they're not there when I can't sleep at night.

I get together with Rigmor only once before summer vacation, when she invites Karen, Børge, their children, and me to see *The Magic Flute* at the Royal Danish Theatre. Just being in the theater takes my breath away. As we're shown to our seats, I twist and turn to take in every detail. It's all so lavish, and once the opera starts, I'm a goner. I had no idea how beautiful opera and classical music could be; I decide right then to buy this one on cassette. Rigmor and I don't get to talk much, but that's all right. The beauty of the opera dampens the terrible loss I feel for Hylleholt and opens me up to the world of classical music. I buy cassette tapes of works by Mozart, Bach, Beethoven, and Handel. I feel a little pang when I buy the last one—my first memories of Mom and Dad are of living on Händelsvej in Copenhagen. That was a lifetime ago. I haven't seen Dad in about four years now and Mom in a year and a half. They probably have no idea where I am. It's not that I don't care, but I'm angry—angry in a terrifying way that gives me dreams about killing Mom. I don't dream about Dad at all anymore.

Summer vacation is rapidly approaching, and I'm frightened at the thought of having seven weeks to myself without school. So I plan to work at the butcher shop every day, except for the week I'm going to that farm with Karen and Børge.

Going on vacation with Karen and Børge means cozy walks in small Swedish villages, swimming in lakes, long conversations at the dinner table, and bonfires—not to mention all that fresh-baked bread. Bolette and I are together from morning till night. She draws while I talk about novels and poems I've read. We wash each other's hair outside at the water pump and go for long walks in the woods.

But something is wrong between Karen and Børge. They seem to be consciously staying on different sides of the house. When we children and Børge are in the front of the house, where there's a sort of court-yard, Karen is sunbathing out back. And when they're finally in the same room, they barely speak to each other. Bolette notices it too. It's one of the things we talk about—that and going to high school. After summer vacation, Bolette is starting tenth grade at my high school, and I'm looking forward to being her "big sister."

As the week passes, the mood becomes increasingly uncomfortable. Børge complains constantly about Karen sunbathing behind the house instead of spending time with us. Karen avoids the confrontation: she doesn't want to fight in front of us. The day we're supposed to go home, it all comes to a head. Børge seems really stressed out while we're packing. Bolette, Anders, and I stand outside by the car and talk.

Suddenly Børge races down the front steps and yells as loudly as he can: "Anders and Bolette—get off your asses and help, you spoiled brats!"

We freeze, all of us staring at him. A shocked smile crosses my face. He adds: "Don't fucking stand there smiling at me!" And then he storms back in.

I'm shaking and fighting to hold back the tears. The old clouds of rage start to gather inside my head, and I decide I'll never speak to him again. If Karen wants to see me, she'll have to come to student housing. Børge no longer exists for me. I pack up the rest of my things frenetically and clean the part of the house that was mine. Ice is running through my veins. Børge, who tries several times to make eye contact, asks me what's wrong. I just stare at him with dead eyes and keep doing what I'm doing. Inside, I'm furious.

Now I have no one at all, I think.

Karen never finds out about the episode, and I don't say anything. But all the way home I'm silent, and when it's time for me to leave I give everyone except Børge a hug. I just stare straight through him. I don't visit them again that summer, but my friendship with both of them ultimately survives their personal difficulties.

I work almost every day at Svendsen's. The shop gets really busy in the summer, thanks to all the people on vacation. Every so often, I look for Klaus, my private-school dance partner, but I don't see him. Not that it means anything. He's just a memory from the summer of my physical awakening, when I screwed my way through scores of men and boys. I'm ashamed I was ever like that.

My psychologist, Mei-Mei, says it's a typical reaction when you've experienced sexual assault. I'm happy she has an explanation, but I think it's weird. Why wouldn't my experiences actually make me afraid of sex? Why would I run the risk of going off with strange men—some of them over thirty—when I knew what it means to be raped? It's as if I were seeking the same dangerous experience. I don't understand why I would do that. All I know is that it made me high; it made me feel chosen. I can still recall the men's surprised and affectionate looks when I did what they asked—what they might have never tried with another girl. I did it all—and they were happy. And I was too, in a strange way.

The days fly by at Svendsen's. We all work up a sweat, and we run more than we walk when we have to get some meat for a customer or bring the dirty dishes out back. We work effectively, all the while chatting and laughing loudly with the customers and each other.

There are a few customers Svendsen prefers serving on his own. Inge-Lise fills me in discreetly the first time I see them in the shop. "These are the boss's customers," she whispers as she walks by, so I don't do anything. One Saturday, a married couple who are two of Svendsen's own comes in. It's past noon and we're closed, but the door is open so we can air the place out while we wash the floor. Svendsen sees them the same time I do, and he goes over to the desk and asks what he can do for them. Turns out they need some meat he'll have to get out of cold storage. They stand there waiting as the rest of us bustle around them trying to clean up. They clearly feel they're in the way. I decide that while they're waiting, I can try to fill the rest of their order: they also need some cold cuts and some salads, which I begin slicing and weighing. While I'm working, I chat a little with the couple. The door to the back room opens, and Svendsen comes out with his arms full of meat. Confused, he stops in his tracks and looks up at me.

"What are you doing, Lisbeth?" he asks.

"I thought I'd help finish up their order while you grabbed the meat," I reply.

He keeps looking at me, his face getting redder. The couple and my coworkers in the shop just stand there staring at me.

"Don't ever do that again," he hisses through his teeth.

At first I'm confused. "What shouldn't I do again?" I ask.

I realize that I just served one of *his* customers. I slowly take my apron and smock off, all the while looking at him. Then I walk right by him into the back room, grab my bag, and go. Furious. How dare he embarrass me that way, in front of customers and my coworkers. I storm down Main Street. I'm through working for such an idiot.

After summer vacation, I start my senior year. I try to turn in A work every day, and I excel among my classmates. I spend all my free time with my friends, and I slowly make even more of them. Teddy gets a new girlfriend—Jeanette—whom I also become good friends with. Bolette starts her sophomore year at the high school. We talk almost every day, and sometimes she even goes back to student housing with me and sleeps over. I teach her how to smoke cigarettes without filters and drink Rioja while we listen to classical music or old Billie Holiday and Louis Armstrong records. And once we're suitably drunk on the red wine, we recite poetry and try to outdo each other with our knowledge of writers. We're invincible—Bolette is the closest thing I'll ever have to a sister.

A month into my senior year, I see her walking toward me in the big schoolyard. Even from a distance, I can tell that something is wrong.

She runs the final few yards and throws herself into my arms, sobbing loudly. I hold her until she calms down.

"What's happened, Bolette?"

"Karen and Børge are getting a divorce."

And then I start crying too. We stand there like that for a long time as confused students pass us by.

"Come on," I say when the bell rings, pulling her into the cafeteria, where we can sit and talk in peace. I light a cigarette and hand it to her.

"What's going to happen now?" I ask. "Who's moving out—and what about you and Anders?"

With tears in her eyes, Bolette tells me that Børge will be staying in the house with the kids and that Karen is moving into their summer cottage. It's Karen who wants the divorce, and Børge is terribly unhappy. Strangely enough, I'm not worried about what effect their divorce will have on my relationship with each of them. I just feel sad for all of them.

Around the same time, I meet Lars. Helle and I are at B & W one night, and he's sitting with a friend on a sofa, watching us dance. During one of the few breaks we take, he asks if I want to dance. I sneak a glance at him. He's handsome and strong. Blond, medium height, smiling eyes, and buff. And he seems sure of himself. Helle dances with his friend Henrik; the rest of the night, the four of us dance around each other. After the bar closes, we head to a bakery to buy fresh-baked breakfast rolls, which we eat in the common kitchen of my building. I suggest we spend the night in my room, and the others agree. My heart pounding, I climb into bed with Lars. Only Teddy—whom I've told about the assaults—has been allowed to touch me in a long time. I feel as if I have a new body that I'm not quite sure what to do with and a newfound fear of sex. So when we crawl beneath the comforters—Henrik and Helle are on a mattress on the floor, and Lars and I are in my bed—I'm stiff and cold all over. Henrik and Helle lie there whispering.

"I wish you could see my pussy," says Helle suddenly.

Helle had gotten a new kitten two days earlier. Lars and I lie quietly listening.

"And you really should see my snake," replies Henrik.

Lars and I burst out laughing—and all my fears seem to vanish. The rest of the night, or morning, to be more accurate, we lie there holding each other. Lars is sleeping, but I'm awake, excited, and happy.

Soon Lars and I are together every hour of the day that we aren't in school or at work. He introduces me to his family: a mother, father, and older brother. His brother is in training at an Irma supermarket, his father is a salesman for Rank Xerox, and his mother runs a toy shop in Haslev, where Lars works. They live in a row house on the outskirts of Haslev, and I'm there so often I almost feel like part of the family. Even though I don't talk that much to his parents, they seem to have accepted me. Sometimes I stop in at the toy shop after school and talk to Lars in the back room, if there aren't any customers. I also sit back there listening to how he and his mother handle customers.

Although Lars makes me happy—and I enjoy every day with him—I'm still connected to Teddy in some special way. Teddy's father died right before we became friends in ninth grade, so I recognize the sense of loss he sometimes talks about. I feel that I've suffered the same loss as Teddy; I think that's what unites us. So we meet sometimes just to have sex, talk, and play. Even though we have our own boyfriend and girlfriend, we continue to disappear, secretly, into a world of tickling each other, putting disgusting things in each other's food, and stealing each other's clothes and hiding them. And then we fall asleep, wrapped around each other. We're like children in a way I've never been with anyone else.

No one knows about my secret relationship with Teddy. I tell Lars we're just friends; he even comes to get me several times after I've spent the night at Teddy's. Everyone thinks it's merely a friendship—and really, except for the sex, which doesn't happen that often, that's what it is. A friendship.

I'm still seeing Mei-Mei every week. The grant money for my therapy sessions has been extended, so I can keep seeing her until I no longer need to. Karen set that up with Ravnsborg township. Once a week I take the train from Haslev to Central Station in Copenhagen, walk out the back entrance and a couple of hundred yards down the street to Halmtorvet, and then up to an apartment on the second floor, where Mei-Mei both lives and works.

I enjoy seeing her. She's calm and talks softly in a charming Faeroese accent. Mei-Mei lives with the sexologist Sten Hegeler, but only on the weekends. She says that breaks are good for a relationship; that way you can give each other some space. I know exactly what she means.

Otherwise she rarely talks about herself. I'm the one who does most of the talking. We slowly review my childhood, year by year, experience by experience. If I try to gloss over the violent episodes, she gently keeps me focused by probing deeper. That works well for me. She doesn't pressure me or say she thinks something is or isn't terrible. She just asks more questions while observing me.

In that way, my treatment is going well—but I soon discover that I can avoid talking about certain things by simply not mentioning them. One of the things I have no desire to tell her—that I've never even told Karen—is the rape I experienced when I was thirteen. I don't know why. Maybe because I don't want them to know me as the Lisbeth I was back then: the embarrassing Lisbeth who was complicit in her own misfortunes. The one who treated people poorly, who stole, drank, and made an ass of herself—just as I did the night that guy raped me.

I like feeling that Mei-Mei perceives me as a proper, intellectual girl who was just unlucky enough to be born into a bad family. Still, I know I was responsible for many things that happened and that I behaved badly in a number of ways. Also, I don't want to destroy her image of me.

This becomes a recurring pattern for me: I don't want to lose face— I don't want to fail again. So I slave over my homework, and when I get a bad grade, I feel totally ashamed. I search to find every possible explanation for why I failed to write the perfect essay or get the highest grade. Usually I conclude it's the teacher's fault. And when I can't prove that, I search high and low for other explanations that will exonerate both me and my performance.

Also, I start turning more attention to my appearance. I replace my entire wardrobe with brand names like Levi's, Kappa, and Lacoste. My style becomes more masculine: I wear my hair short and dress in polo shirts buttoned all the way up, with pullovers on top, and docksides on my feet. And I'm always in pants—never dresses. I prefer dressing like the boys at Herlufsholm. Now and then, Helle and Marianne try to get me to dress a little more "girly," but when I acquiesce and put on more frilly things, I'm uncomfortable. Any clothes that show my curves are out: they make me feel ugly and unattractive. I spend more energy hiding my body than accentuating it. I'm convinced that my appearance has to signal ambition and strength.

Because I don't like the real Lisbeth and the environment she comes from, I construct an image of the person I'd like to be. I work hard at becoming known as ambitious and anarchistic Lisbeth, someone others admire and fear. I don't need them to love me—but they have to admire me.

I often discuss my anger issues with Mei-Mei. I can be standing in line at the supermarket or in the middle of a discussion in class and suddenly feel the uncontrollable urge to explode. Even though I don't, rage smolders within me. I use words instead: quick, cutting remarks and ridicule are my preferred weapons—and those who know me also know they had better be ready to go the whole nine yards. I don't stop until my opponent has tears in her eyes and shuts up. It provides immediate satisfaction and a way to vent my anger.

Mei-Mei tries to help me understand the source of all this anger, which also surfaces whenever I have nightmares. In them, I'm always guilty of causing death, in one way or another, or of physically harming my mother. I'm either running her down with a car or, more commonly, beating her with my bare fists or a stick.

Mei-Mei assures me that it's completely normal, considering my upbringing. Still, I can't understand why I'm dreaming of killing my mother when she's the one who's always been beaten by her men. I don't want anyone else to discover this frightening side of me.

Now and then I dream about both Jan and Mogens and what they did to me. In my dreams, Jan usually consummates the sex—and I want him to. I often wake up sexually aroused. At the same time, I want to throw up. It's disgusting to be dreaming like that, and I hate myself—and my body—for reacting in that way.

I never wanted Jan to assault me. Nevertheless, when Mei-Mei and I discuss my experiences, I discover that some small part of me appreciated the intimacy it provided. At the time, it made me feel that someone—even if it was Jan—liked me. I would never have been able to admit it to myself, but with Mei-Mei's help, I can accept the thought that it was one way for a neglected girl to feel intimacy, maybe even a kind of love. That's why I never protested or resisted—why I didn't sleep in that strange room out back when we were in Torrig, why I kept sleeping in the same room as Mom and Jan. I'm ashamed and hate myself for not refusing back then.

After sessions like this with Mei-Mei, I'm exhausted and I shake with chills. The only thing I want is a hot dog, a Coke, and the train to

Haslev; I fall asleep as soon as I sit down. Thank God all our sessions aren't this difficult. Sometimes I feel as if I'm discussing things with Mei-Mei that I could have discussed with a mother. By the time the train reaches Haslev, I'm thrilled that Lars is there to pick me up at the station and that I won't be alone in student housing.

Mei-Mei and I talk about Mom and Dad too. I'm still determined not to see Mom. The very thought of her makes me physically ill, and my dreams about hurting her scare the hell out of me. However, the reason I won't see my father becomes increasingly unclear to me. I tell Mei-Mei about being angry that he sent the police after me when I was thirteen and let them drive me in a police car from Copenhagen to Nakskov. She asks if Dad tried to get me himself before contacting the police.

"Yes," I say, my eyes filled with angry tears.

"Then what else could he have done when you wouldn't go with him? He knew it wasn't good for you to be living with your brother," she says quietly.

That settles it. The next day I call information from a pay phone in student housing and ask for his telephone number, and then I call him.

"Hi, it's Lisbeth." I hold my breath.

"Oh, hi, Lisbeth. Good to hear from you," he says. He asks where I'm living and what I'm doing. He's living on Amager with a woman named Åse who has two small children. Kenneth is also living with him, whereas Tommy and Susan are living with Anita. Even though they're divorced now, everything's fine between him and Anita. I ask about my brothers. He doesn't know where René and Michael are; the only thing he knows is that Michael and Kirsten aren't together anymore, and the twins are with her. Tonny's in Horsens State Penitentiary, where he's serving a six-and-a-half-year sentence for armed robbery. That upsets me—Tonny is only twenty-one and he's already been in jail for a few years.

We decide to meet the next week at Café Klaptræet in Copenhagen, when I'll be in town again to see Mei-Mei. As I hang up, I feel giddy and happy.

I call the prison, which informs me that Tonny has to send me a visitor permission form; so I write to Tonny and tell him I want to visit him in Horsens.

The following week I meet Dad in the city. He's already at the restaurant when I arrive. I recognize him the minute I see him. He looks like himself, except a little heavier. I still think he's handsome. When he sees me and stands up to give me a hug, I'm happy. Inside, I know it's foolish to feel that way—what has he ever really done for me? He's partially culpable for my brothers' and my own wretched childhoods, but I'm just so thrilled to see him again.

He says he's proud of me and glad we've gotten together. We discuss a number of topics: which classes I like, how Lars is doing, how Åse is. We don't mention the day he sent the police after me. I don't want to talk about it. Partially because I'm embarrassed over how I was at that time, and partially because I don't want to ruin the good vibe between us. We share a delightful evening—and right before we part, we decide that he's going to host my eighteenth birthday party a month later.

By the time I get home, I'm feeling elated. I've seen Dad for the first time in four years—and in a month we'll celebrate my birthday at Dad's row house on Amager. I can bring Marianne and Lars with me, and Dad will invite Anita, her new husband, and my half siblings.

The day I turn eighteen, Lars wakes me up with morning buns and gifts. Karen and Børge call to wish me happy birthday, and in the afternoon, Marianne, Lars, and I head to Amager. Åse is young and quite thin—she says nothing. Dad is busy in the kitchen. We help him make

Hasselback potatoes, and we're going to have rump roast too. I chatter away about how to carve meat, conveniently avoiding how my time at Svendsen's ended.

Anita and her new husband, Jens, along with my three young half siblings, show up a little later. Kenneth is thirteen now, Tommy is eleven, and Susan is six. Kenneth, who's wearing glasses, sits there talking like an adult, and Tommy, who still has wispy white baby hair, keeps racing around the table and hitting all of us on the head with a dessert spoon. Susan, the loveliest little girl, has long hair, big blue almond-shaped eyes, and a pouty mouth. Her dress is all ruffles and shades of pink. I watch her on the sly. It's so unfair—the only difference between Susan and me is that I was born from a different mother. She was born into pink happiness. Her parents may be divorced, but I know Anita. For her, the children always come first.

At one point when the others have left the table, Susan and I talk.

"You look so pretty with that long hair," I tell her.

"I know," she replies.

I feel so jealous of her.

It's a wonderful evening, despite any thoughts about how my life would have been if I'd had a different mother and father. That night I head home with Lars and Marianne, happy and full.

The time approaches when I need to start thinking about my higher education. I can't stand the thought of going to college without knowing what I'm going to study, so I need to decide now. I want a degree that will lead to a job: something demanding and totally different than what the others in my class will be studying.

I borrow *What Can I Become?* and spend a couple of evenings plowing through the book. It includes unemployment rates for all degrees, which I review carefully. Political economy and law have the lowest rates, and both degrees seem tough. So, I decide to pursue both.

Political economy involves a lot of mathematics—one track has extra mathematics for people who majored in linguistics in high school. Still, I figure that's no problem.

Spring flies by, and school becomes increasingly stressful. All of us realize that this semester really matters, so I'm doing homework constantly. I often sit up all night writing papers, but I don't mind. I have to find some way to get through all the nightmares, so schoolwork helps to pass the time. In general, I'm doing well, though I'm never satisfied with my efforts. I always feel I could have done better if I'd worked even harder.

I focus solely on school. I'm not a very good girlfriend; I fall asleep while we're watching films together, and sex is rarely in the cards. I'm putting all my energy into getting the diploma I just plain need.

The day finally arrives for me to wear my cap and gown. Just as I'm about to take my orals in German—my last exam—Karen shows up at school; she's wearing a nice dress and carrying a rose. I'm ridiculously nervous. My other orals have all gone well, without incident, but I'm really nervous about this last exam, even though German is now one of my best subjects. I stammer and stutter through it and wind up with a B-minus. Any disappointment with my efforts disappears immediately as Karen, tears in her eyes, hands me my cap and gown. I have no idea what the other students are thinking: I'm standing here with my social worker, while everyone else has their family with them. In this moment, however, it doesn't matter. For me, Karen is the only one who should be giving me my graduation cap.

I didn't tell Dad when I would be graduating—in fact, I didn't even invite him to the party Karen and Børge are throwing for me. Neither he nor Mom is responsible for how I've managed to make it this far, so I don't see why he should be here celebrating my accomplishments. Despite a wonderful birthday and our renewed contact, I'm still angry about his betrayal. Also, I've already decided that if I ever get married, he won't be the one walking me down the aisle.

However, Rigmor, Karen, Bolette, Anders, and Lars are here to help me celebrate. During the luncheon, Rigmor gives a speech in which she discusses my long journey from that fourteen-year-old girl arriving at Hylleholt until now. She concludes by saying she's proud of me—and proud that Hylleholt managed to take a student all the way to her diploma. I'm proud too. I wish I had done better than my B average, but Rigmor's ceremonious speech makes me realize I've accomplished something rare.

The day arrives for the traditional horse and carriage that drives groups of graduates from home to home. I've already informed them that we won't be driving by mine. I could have easily asked Karen and Børge, but I haven't. So, on this day I ride around to all the other students' homes and parents. I'm just happy that all the festivities eclipse the fact that we won't be driving by my home or seeing my parents.

This year I'm not afraid of summer vacation. I have Lars and my friends, and I need to prep for all the studying I'll soon be doing. I've decided to go on living in Haslev, even though I'm attending the University of Copenhagen. It'll take me an hour each way by train, but I'll spend the time reading, so that's not a problem. To be honest, I can't handle trying to find an apartment in Copenhagen. Thank God Karen's already procured the necessary money for me: I've been given funding for housing for all six years, so I won't have to live solely off the state education grant.

Getting my high school diploma was one of the greatest moments of my life. Although I went on to get a college degree, my high school graduation was even more important. In this picture I'm opening gifts at Karen and Børge's, right before the luncheon where Rigmor spoke.

I've been in therapy for over a year now, but I don't feel in any way ready to stop the weekly sessions.

I'm still having violent nightmares, I'm still haunted by shame, and I'm never satisfied with my performance. Mei-Mei assures me repeatedly that I'm accomplishing the superhuman almost every day, but I know I could do even better if I were more diligent. Once I start college, my plan is to work my ass off from the very first day—and that worries Mei-Mei.

She works hard at trying to get me to relax and enjoy life now and then—to learn how to fail and shrug it off. I already enjoy life, but shrugging it off is just not me. I'm grateful for what the township, Mei-Mei, Karen, and Hylleholt have done for me. To waste all that support by being lazy would make me sick, which I tell Mei-Mei in no uncertain terms. What I don't tell her is that if I don't keep at it until I taste blood, everyone will find out how dumb and bad I really am.

When the envelope from the university finally arrives at the end of July, I tear it open. I've been accepted as a political economy major. Law was my top choice, but my grade point average is .02 too low to get in. Still, I decide to be happy I'm going to be a political economy major, where my GPA is far above what's necessary. I call Karen immediately to tell her the good news.

"Congratulations!" she yells into the receiver. "So you're going to become an economist. Maybe you'll be prime minister someday."

"No way," I say, laughing loudly. "I don't want to become a politician—I want to make money!"

Karen asks about practical matters: When do I start classes? Do I have to buy new books? Have I gotten a season ticket for the train? Although I'm on top of all that already, I ask her to find out if I can get a grant from the township to buy books. I've forgotten that once I turn eighteen, Karen is no longer my guardian. She never told me that I would have to take care of those things on my own once I became an adult—and she doesn't tell me now either. She just says: "Yes, we'll have to look into that. I'll get back to you shortly."

The next time I go to see Mei-Mei, I pass by Frue Plads first. I open the gigantic wooden door of the University of Copenhagen's main building and slip inside. The entrance hall is covered with paintings and wood carvings, just like the Royal Danish Theatre. Fortunately there aren't any other people around. Mustering my courage, I tiptoe up one of the two grand staircases and enter a hallway with a lot of tall doors and a hardwood floor that creaks loudly as you walk on it. My heart is pounding—I'm afraid someone's going to toss me out of there. Calming down, I try to slow my heartbeat as I breathe in the atmosphere.

I start college on the first of September, 1986. All the new students— there must be a hundred of us—meet on Studiestræde, a street in Copenhagen. I look around at all the stylish guys and girls: they remind me of the guys from Herlufsholm. At least half of the girls have their hair in a dyed pageboy, and many of the boys are wearing recently ironed shirts. I'm in my obligatory polo shirt and pullover, so I fit right in (though I look more like a boy than a girl). I'm not wearing makeup anymore, and I haven't been shaving my legs or armpits, or plucking my eyebrows. Mei-Mei says I hide my femininity because it makes me feel safe.

Some older students—advisors to the freshmen—are holding up signs showing our different group numbers. The guy holding up the sign for my group looks different from many of the others. Tall and thin, with a mass of wild hair, he's wearing an Icelandic sweater and worn jeans. As we walk toward my group's locale, I try to stay near him. Peter—that's his name—lives in a leftist collective, is active in student politics, and is a member of the Communist party. He comes from an academic family in Holte: his mother is a French teacher at a private school, his father is an engineer and fine artist, and his little brother is studying art history. Peter is seven years older than me, and I'm totally in love from the moment I lay eyes on him.

The next three weeks fly by as I start my courses; I'm dead tired every afternoon when I arrive back in Haslev. We see our student advisors several times a week at social events. I try to stay close to Peter, though I'm not sure he even notices me.

After three weeks of school, freshmen spend three days of orientation in a cabin out in the country. The others in my group are sweet enough; there's a pretty wide age difference between me, definitely the youngest, and the oldest, who's thirty. I don't spend much time getting to know the others during orientation. I'm far more interested in Peter—and the feeling turns out to be mutual. The first night, almost everyone gets drunk, including Peter and me. Before we know it, we're sitting together exchanging book titles as if we were playing cards. Peter has read a lot more books than I have, but we've read a number of the same titles. We spend half the night talking about these books and what they've meant to us. The others quickly abandon the conversation, until finally only he and I are left talking into the night. The next night, we do more than talk; we also kiss. By the time orientation is over, Peter and I are officially seeing each other.

Back in Haslev, I tell Lars that I've met someone else. He's sad about it but our parting is undramatic. I've been pretty removed, both mentally and physically, and I think he had an inkling it was coming.

From here on, I'm only in Haslev to wash clothes and check my mail. Otherwise I'm with Peter at his collective, where I meet a number of older intellectual students. Peter introduces me to the world of student politics, and before long I'm elected to student council.

Peter and I share our passion for literature, and it turns out he has as large a collection of comic books as Karen and Børge. He also has the most records I've ever seen, all of them jazz, classical, and blues. I knew nothing about blues before, but now I'm totally hooked.

I'm happy. I learn everything I can from Peter during the day, and at night we make love quietly and intensely. Any problems I've had with intimacy and security are gone, or at least minimized. I surrender and enjoy life. One night while we're lying there whispering in the dark, we decide to move in together. I've only been in college for two months, but I feel as if I've awakened in another life. Helle introduces me to someone she knows in Haslev who has an apartment to rent in Copenhagen. Two weeks later, Peter and I move into our own apartment in Nørrebro.

We start to form study groups at college. I'm in a group with Mikael, who's a few years older than me, and Lise, who's ten years older. Mikael, a dreamer and an opera buff, introduces me to Maria Callas and other female opera singers. We go to the opera together and watch operas on film at Park Bio cinema. Mikael becomes my new best friend. Lise, the most mature of the three of us, runs our reading group while teaching Mikael and me about matrices, vectors, and calculating probability. Math has never come easy to me—and in political economy, I encounter concepts and formulas I've never heard of. Suddenly the Greek alphabet has become an integral part of my everyday life in the worst way: the letters appear in every single formula we have to learn.

Even though he's three years ahead of me, I can't rely on Peter for help with math. To him, math was just something you survived—and the grade was irrelevant. The first time I complain about how hard it is, he laughs. He says that in political economy I have to just get through subjects like math, microeconomics, and financing—and that I can't expect high grades. He tells me that most people fail a few subjects, which isn't a problem, and that I probably will too. I can't fathom failing any class; so, with Mikael and Lise as my buddy and mentor, respectively, I work my ass off studying math and the Greek alphabet.

During summer vacation, Tonny had answered my letter. He writes like someone in fourth grade; I'm shocked at how poorly he spells. He's understandable, though, and I can tell he's happy to hear from family. He also sends a visitor's pass, which I fill out. I have permission to visit him now, as long as I set it up beforehand with the prison. One Friday afternoon, I take the train to Horsens. I've brought along my old boom box, so he can hear some music in his cell, a five-hundred-kroner note, and a pack of King's. That's what he asks for. He also writes that I have to open the pack of cigarettes and tell the guard that I smoke. Oh, and I need to put the kroner note deep down in my pocket.

I do as he asks. Actually, I stopped smoking the first month Peter and I were together, but I have no problem saying I still smoke.

When I arrive at the jail, which lies on the outskirts of town, they inspect my bag and jacket, and I'm body-searched. They don't find the money. They take away the boom box to inspect it more closely, but the officers promise me that Tonny will get it. Even though they're very nice, I still feel like a suspect and a criminal by the time they show me to the visitor cell. There are bars on the high windows, and the walls are white and shabby. There's a wooden table with a pair of chairs and a cot with a folded sheet and towel on it. It's disgusting to think that they'd put a sheet out even though it's Tonny's sister who's visiting.

By the time they finally bring Tonny into the room, along with a pot of coffee and two mugs, I'm really uncomfortable. It vanishes like dew in the sunshine, however, the moment I see him. Tonny, who's unbelievably happy to see me, gives me a big hug. Five years have passed since we last saw each other, and he's really changed. He's wearing a white undershirt and jeans, and he's completely bald. He has tattoos on both arms and his back, and a ring in one eyebrow and in both ears. His muscles are bulging. He lifts weights every day, so he can take care of himself if anyone comes after him. Although it's wonderful to see him, there's something scary about him. His voice is filled with hate when he talks about immigrants and admiration when he talks about bikers.

Barely ten minutes go by before he asks about the cigarettes and money. I hand him both. He pulls the plastic off the pack of cigarettes, rolls the five-hundred-kroner bill tightly, puts it down into the plastic, and then spins it around until it becomes thin and elongated. Then he opens his pants, bends forward a little, and sticks it up his rectum. He quickly closes his pants again as he laughs and says he hopes he isn't chosen for a rectal inspection. I'm shocked. I had no idea that's what it means to be an inmate and that's how they smuggle things in.

During the visit, which lasts about an hour, Tonny tells me about his life and the friends and environment that are costing him so many years in prison. When the hour is over, I promise I'll visit him again once I've saved up enough money. This visit cost me more than a thousand kroner, so I can't do it very often. I half run back to the center of Horsens to catch the train; I feel sick and sad—as if everyone can see that I've just been to the prison.

Back home, I tell Peter about the visit. As we share a bottle of red wine, I talk in great detail about my upbringing and my family, including the assaults. He's not shocked. I also tell him that I don't see Mom anymore, but while I'm saying it, I suddenly get the urge to see her again—to show her what my life is like now, and to show her I've become an adult. I tell Peter, who encourages me to call her. I dial her number, and after it rings a few times, she answers.

"Hi, Mouse!" she exclaims when she hears my voice.

A second later she's telling me that she got a new refrigerator and what she and Richard had to eat yesterday. I ask if she'd like to visit me at Mjølnerparken housing project one day.

"Of course, honey. Let me just find out when Richard can come with me"—which reminds her that Richard just grilled some eel, and she asks if she should bring some with them.

"Yes, Mom, bring the eel with you," I say, smiling.

Not a word about why she hasn't seen me in two years. No questions about what I'm doing now. Not that I'd expected it. I'm just happy that Peter and Mom will get to meet and that I'll see her again. Things are what they are, and I'm mature enough now to make my peace with them.

After all, I'm almost nineteen.

EPILOGUE

Lucky stars and fairy tales
I'm gonna bathe myself in a wishin' well
Pretty scars from cigarettes
I never will forget, I never will forget

I'm still afraid to be alone
Wish that moon would follow me home
I leave the light on
I leave that light on
I ain't that bad I'm just messed up
I ain't that sad but I'm sad enough

—Beth Hart: "Leave the Light On"

I love Beth Hart's lyrics. *Leave the Light On* is always playing on my car's CD player before I have to speak about my childhood. It puts me in the right frame of mind.

I didn't realize until I was forty-three and reconnected with Grethe and Otto that my arms were covered in cigarette burns when the nine-year-old me went home with them. I'd forgotten that—yet it's Beth Hart's lyrics about the scars from cigarettes I've sung along with most in the car. I've asked Mom if she remembers them; she doesn't. Nor does she remember the sexual assaults or the day the bus from the orphanage came to get me as I screamed I hated her.

What she does remember is the cost of the beer she and Richard bought at the local bar in Nørrebro when we reunited after two years had gone by.

It has been a fact of life for me that Mom only remembers or notices what matters to her. I've learned to live with that. No, not just live with it—I've learned to embrace her and give her the kind of care she never received as a child. I just spent a week in Bulgaria with her and my children. It was our first vacation together ever, and it went well. She was just like one of the children, with the same rules and freedoms. Does it sound a little strange? Not for Mom and me.

Reading the end of the book, you might think everything was fine: "And they lived happily ever after." That was not the case. Still, in my late teens I built a foundation that has helped me through the rest of my life, helped me live with very serious psychological scars, helped me to live a good life. Throughout my adolescence, I learned from all my mentors that life must be consumed and enjoyed, not merely gotten through. At the age of fifty-one, I feel I'm almost there.

Recently, I awakened early one morning in a state of euphoria. I woke up my husband, yet another Mikael, to tell him I had envisioned growing old—and that I wanted to. It was a whole new feeling. When I was in my twenties, I dreamed one night that I would die when I was thirty-five. So, I made my peace with it. When I was hospitalized with a critical illness—fourteen days before I turned thirty-six—I knew that my dream would come true. Ole, my husband at the time, knew about my dream and was deeply unhappy. As he and my friends gathered around my hospital bed, I knew the time had come. I was totally calm. My only concern was how to explain to my children that I was leaving them prematurely. It was an unbearable sorrow to have to leave them. Still, I took comfort in the fact that I had chosen the best parents they could have—Peter and Ole.

Although I was operated on immediately, the surgeon couldn't figure out what was wrong. That night Fatina grabbed hold of me. She massaged, stroked, chanted, and beseeched me back to life. I lay in bed with a J-pouch that wasn't working and a body swollen with waste it couldn't get rid of. Suddenly illness and death released their grasp on me. Fatina got my innards to flow again, and in a few days, I was back on my feet. Since then I've sent her grateful thoughts every single day.

Suddenly I was facing a life that would be much longer than I'd expected—I felt a constant anxiety about it until that morning I woke up Mikael. The difference is the book you're holding in your hands. For me, writing my way through the first eighteen years of my life has been more life-affirming than anything I've ever experienced. Now what matters most is dying old, satiated by life, and surrounded by a sea of children, grandchildren, and great-grandchildren.

MY FAMILY AND ME TODAY

Today, my life resembles most people's. I have a wonderful, busy schedule with five children, a career, and a husband. I have a close circle of friends, mostly the people you've met in this book: Karen, Børge, Fatina, and Bolette. I also have a somewhat larger circle of friends who aren't quite as close, including Jeanette, Helle, Marianne, Teddy, and others from my time in Faxe Ladeplads and Haslev. Over the course of time more people have come into my life.

I'm far from the ideal friend: I often forget my friends' birthdays—in fact, sometimes I forget that they even exist. It's not out of malice or indifference; my friends know that they need to nudge me now and then to get my attention.

I've thought a lot about why I forget the people I care about. If I were an electrical system, you'd find a loose connection somewhere inside me. If you were to wiggle the wire that's not working properly, the lights would blink a few times and then the power would return for a while. I'm glad that it's only a loose connection that has to be prodded a little to get the feelings to come back. It could be much worse: I could be permanently disconnected. Still, now and then I experience a blockage that makes me unaware of anyone except my children and my husband, Mikael. On the other hand, I'm constantly aware of *them*—it's only my friends who sometimes disappear from view.

I've discovered a term for it: "attachment disorder." My brothers, my mother, and I all suffer from it, to varying degrees. Our ability to establish bonds with other people has been more or less destroyed (mine a little less than the rest of the family). So, I'm able to both fall in love with someone and love my children, but it takes years for me to connect with anyone else. It will probably never be a strong bond—but the more ties that bind us, the more likely it is that the connection will become a strong one.

Sometimes a thread breaks, especially if a comment—or even just a look—from a friend hurts or angers me. Then my warm feelings disappear, and all that remains is coldness and the old urge to kill. Eventually, I'll laugh a little at myself. Still, up to half a year can pass before I'm willing to accept an outstretched hand from the one who erred. It's foolish, I know, but once I remember to tell my friends that it's just a flaw in me that they have to overlook, they soon forgive me. Actually, I haven't banished anyone from my life in recent years.

I'm fiercely attached to my children, a feeling that began the moment I became pregnant with Asbjørn. About a year after we met, Peter and I decided to have a child—a love child. I became pregnant in February of 1988, when I turned twenty, and Asbjørn came into the world on November 29. I never questioned having a child—or whether Peter would make a good father. I had more concerns about my abilities as a mother, though I didn't share them with anyone.

Still, I knew I could make a perfect mother (anything less would be unacceptable). So I went to the library and systematically worked my way through the literature about pregnancy and children up to the age of eighteen. I tore through both academic and popular books on the subject; during the course of my pregnancy, I became a font of wisdom on pregnancy and childbirth. I also attended prenatal classes with Peter, and I ate and drank in a way that would result in giving birth to the model child. Long before I gave birth, I had everything in place. I knitted lanolin-rich woolen trousers, and we purchased a washing machine so that Asbjørn could have ecological and pH-balanced cloth diapers instead of harmful disposable ones. The baby sling was also ready to go. I carried him in it right from the start, because I wanted him to feel closeness and love all day long.

The birth did not go as expected: after more than two days of labor pains in the maternity ward, I had to have an emergency C-section to deliver Asbjørn. Because I never complained about the pain, they started calling me "that tough chick from Lolland." I had horrible pain—just like everyone else—I just didn't want anyone to find out about it.

As soon as Asbjørn was born, I started worrying that something might happen to him. If I had to cross a street or ride in an elevator with him, I would get panic attacks and feel as if I were going to pass out. I started avoiding all situations that might place him in any possible danger. The first time we gave him solid food, I was terrified he might get something stuck in his throat. When he got sick, I couldn't sleep, and if he became fidgety, I'd walk the floor with him, positive that something was seriously wrong.

A few months after I gave birth, I was emaciated: I weighed less than a hundred pounds. Although I was constantly exhausted, I never told anyone about it, not even Peter. I knew I wasn't suffering from postpartum depression, at least not one that had anything to do with Asbjørn. Quite the opposite—he was the love of my life. He was in my thoughts constantly; my only concern was his well-being. I nursed him around the clock, and he grew into a gigantic baby. In fact, I kept nursing him until he was two and a half years old. He was the one who wanted to stop.

It destroyed my relationship with Peter. I disappeared for him—and he for me. I spent all my time on Asbjørn and my studies; I never even took a leave of absence. I carried Asbjørn with me to lectures, and if classmates asked me to go out with them, he was always with me.

Diapers in my backpack, milk in my breasts, Asbjørn in his sling, and off I went. He became my entire life in an unhealthy way—I'm just glad that he wasn't scarred by the constant attention of such an obsessive mother. Peter was a healthy counterpoint, insisting on being part of Asbjørn's life, which I'm extremely thankful for today. For me, Peter was the perfect role model for how a father takes care of his child.

When I was twenty-two and Asbjørn was two, I ended my relationship with Peter. We just didn't exist for each other any longer. I was constantly unhappy—and I was making him unhappy. We shared joint custody of Asbjørn, who spent equal time between us—one week with me, one with Peter. Fortunately, we became good at sharing custody; I'm certain that Karen and Børge's divorce helped me see that it could be done the right way.

During the weeks Asbjørn spent with Peter, I would wither inside. I struggled to find joy in my studies and in seeing friends. I took frequent walks around Damhus Lake, which we had moved close to, wondering who would miss me if I no longer existed. Only Asbjørn, I thought. The old loneliness from my days in student housing would flare up again, some days so strongly that I couldn't get out of bed. Peter and I had moved into a collective, and Peter chose to move out when we separated. Although it was a gift for me to be living with people I knew cared for me, it did nothing to erase my loneliness. At college, I found a new boyfriend, which helped to fill my days and give my life some meaning, but every other week, I felt as if I were dying.

On the other hand, I felt reborn whenever Asbjørn came home again. I organized my days so that he and I could be together as much as possible. He was everything for me when he was home.

Now and then the people around me would point out that I was protecting him too much and not setting boundaries. I was baffled: Asbjørn never came anywhere near my boundaries. He was the most delightful child you could imagine, and he continues to be so delightful as an adult. Now he's an officer in the Royal Danish Life Guards, which no one could have foreseen, considering how overprotective I was. Asbjørn has developed into a strong, warm person, always in balance, and I'm happy he survived having me for a mother. Last year—on my mother's birthday—he made me a grandma with the birth of Harald, a mini-version of Asbjørn.

After being alone with Asbjørn for two years, I decided I wanted more children and a good father for them. So I returned to one of my old methods, but with a new objective. I asked Mom if she'd like to go into the city with me—she was forty-eight at this time and still attractive—and she agreed. My plan was to systematically investigate all possibilities for finding a suitable father for my future children.

It happened quickly. Our first night in the city, I met Ole, and within a few days we knew we were going to have a family together. We used to joke that I must have checked out his bank account, pay stubs, and teeth before I chose him (and there was a grain of truth in that). I'd already decided I wanted to find the world's best father for my children, which also meant a decent person, one with a handle on things. Ole proved to be not only a decent person but also one of the most gifted and warm people I'd ever met. We moved in together, and within six years we had four children.

First came Ida. I was worried that I'd obsess about her in the same way I had with Asbjørn. With Ole in my life, however, my constant fear about Asbjørn's well-being vanished; they loved each other's company. Ole and Peter also became good friends, and the three of us would get together often (which is still true). I was in an entirely different mental state when Ida was born. I was much more in balance, which was good because Ida had colic. I don't know if I could have handled that with Asbjørn: I would have blamed myself. Together, Ole and I comforted Ida through the difficult months, which finally ended when she went on the bottle. It turned out I was starving her because I wasn't producing enough milk. That would have demolished me in the past; now I was able to shrug it off and feel happy we'd found the source of the problem. It wasn't at all shameful.

One year and twenty-six days later, Freja arrived. A few days before Ole and I married, I'd discovered I was pregnant again. Ida was only four months old. We were happy; I felt invincible as a mom. This is what I always wanted in life—and I found out I was good at it. When Freja was born, it was like having twins. We worked hard to make the family function on a daily basis, but I always felt a rush of joy about my children.

When Tea showed up three years later, her three siblings, Ole, and I were already waiting happily. I was turning into a kind of baby machine, and a few days after giving birth, Tea and I came home to four sets of open arms and tons of sibling affection. It was wonderful to see how much tenderness Asbjørn, Ida, and Freja exhibited toward Tea. Tea was number four, just as I was, which reminded me of the tenderness my brothers once felt for me.

A year and a half later, I became pregnant again. Unfortunately I miscarried, which was a great loss for Ole and me. We decided to try again, though, and two years after Tea's birth, Magnus completed our plan of having a large, happy family. We showered Magnus with so much affection that he sometimes ran screaming in the other direction. Still, I knew you couldn't get too much love, so I didn't worry.

When I met Ole, I was writing my thesis; at twenty-four, I was one of the youngest graduate students in my program. My old fear began to rear its ugly head: I was certain people would discover that I was incompetent and that I'd never get a job. At one point, I stayed in bed for two straight weeks. I couldn't shower or eat—and I couldn't answer the phone without crying. In retrospect, I must have been in a deep state of depression, but I never talked to anyone about it. Not even Karen. I had stopped seeing Mei-Mei a little earlier, when I first became pregnant.

Although the others in my collective sensed that something was wrong, they didn't get involved. The prospect of Asbjørn's return each week was the only thing that got me out of bed. I might have been a zombie, but I managed to start eating, bathing, and writing.

Ole protected me and took care of practical matters as I sat buried in industrial economics and game theory. I turned in my thesis and received a B for a "sober review of existing models without adding any new research to the theory." I was relieved—in my mind, it was a miracle I had even gotten that far.

Despite all my fears and concerns, I got a job with Codan Insurance and started learning how to program by taking courses at IBM. Bitten by the programming bug, I soon sought employment at Danske Bank, which offered even more possibilities. At that point, I was twenty-six, pregnant again, and totally inexperienced. Still, Danske Bank wanted me anyway, and that position became a hallmark of my career. Despite pregnancies and maternity leaves, I've been promoted repeatedly: even as a new mom to child number five, I was offered a good management job at KMD, one of the leading IT firms in Denmark.

At KMD, I became a workaholic, so much so that I was working whenever I wasn't with the children—and sometimes simultaneously. I had increasingly less time for Ole, and one day we had to face facts and admit that our dream of having a family together no longer meant living together. At that point, we'd known each other for thirteen years. I was—unequivocally—the one who destroyed our marriage. As with Peter, Ole disappeared for me, and I for him. It had started to become a pattern. We broke up, and I moved into an apartment nearby. Since then, the children have split their time between Ole and me; we've been each other's best friends and solid parents. Today, Mikael and Ole also have their own friendship.

That's the way it's always been for me: ever since I left Faxe Ladeplads, the boys and men who've really meant something have stayed in my life. I'm grateful for all of them.

When Tea was still an infant, I discovered that I had a chronic illness: I started bleeding out of my rectum. A long time passed before I said anything to anyone, but finally it became so bad that I had to tell Ole. At this point, I couldn't sit in a two-hour meeting without taking a break midway so I could "bleed." I underwent a series of examinations and was finally diagnosed with ulcerative colitis.

I wasn't really surprised: I'd always felt I was in bad health, but as with my pregnancies, I was determined not to let it control my life. I've always felt I was just a head—my body a mere appendage—and nothing was going to interfere with my head. I was beyond pain: I'd developed that skill early on. Maybe because of the affronts my body had suffered; maybe as a consequence of having to handle illness on my own in my childhood. I'd had stomachaches from as far back as I could remember.

Years of immunosuppressive and anti-inflammatory medicine followed my diagnosis. I was downing more than twenty pills a day. My face swelled up from the adrenocortical hormones, and I slept at most for five hours a night. Often I'd get up at four in the morning and start working on the computer. At this time, one promotion and raise followed another—I was high on success. Ole tried to get through to me, but I shut him down with accusations of resenting my success.

One day I called to tell him he needed to come and get me. I couldn't feel my legs. Magnus was about two at the time. We drove to Herlev Hospital, where I was admitted with extremely low blood pressure and a fever of 104 Fahrenheit. For four days, they pumped me full of adrenocortical hormones. I brought my computer with me, however, and asked that work arrive with my daily mail. So, I handled my IT projects from my hospital bed—when I wasn't walking up and down the stairs from the twelfth floor to the lobby to shake the discomfort out of my body.

I didn't get better, though, and I wound up having an operation where they removed my large intestine and I was given an ileostomy. Am I better now? Well, at the time I wrote this, I'd just undergone another operation because of an inflamed gallbladder and yet another to remove my stoma. Am I any wiser now? I know I have to take my poor health into account—but I also know that I can do whatever I want. I don't let my physical well-being dictate what I can accomplish. That's a survival skill I acquired in my childhood, and if I use it moderately today, it doesn't kill me—it only makes me stronger.

I still need to tell you about my family today. When he was thirty-nine, René committed suicide. I read about it in the local paper in Nakskov. His life had been full of ups and downs. Mostly, he worked as a waiter and insulator, but over time he became an alcoholic and sick from HIV; he wound up in the bushes beneath his window, pumped full of alcohol and medicine. The delivery boy found him the next morning. According to my father, René had called the police the day before to tell them he was going to commit suicide.

After we became adults, I didn't see much of René. We'd meet now and then, for example when he and Hanne had their daughter Natascha, who's the same age as Asbjørn, or when he married Annette. I still see Natascha, and I try to pass on as much knowledge about her father as I can—which isn't much. When René and I met, it usually ended in quarrels. They were usually my fault; I would get furious with him for wasting his talents and his life. Although René was bright, he repeatedly destroyed everything for himself and those closest to him because of his drinking. René and I were the most similar—with a little more willpower and help from some adults, he could have had a life at least as good as mine. It used to make me furious.

Tonny lives near Mikael, Ole, and me, and we all take care of him. Tonny has AIDS, among other complications from drug abuse and drinking. He's on early retirement and receives daily help from the township, but he seems to be doing quite well. He still takes his daily walk to buy beer, and he participates in all our family gatherings. He's everyone's Uncle Tonny. One day Ida said that Uncle Tonny is like a big brother who hasn't taken care of himself. The children feel great concern for him.

I help him stay in touch with his daughter, Janina, whom he had with a woman named Charlotte. They broke up shortly after Janina's birth, and then everything went to hell for Tonny. During the following years, he was in and out of prison and involved with Bandidos and other gangs. Ole has even participated in negotiations for payment of extortion fines to Bandidos.

Tonny and I have never become furious with each other, whereas René and I had. I never expected that Tonny would do well.

Michael is a chapter in and of himself. Monkey—as we still call him—was and always will be my big brother, with a capital *B*. He used to call me "darling" when we'd meet, and I would become four years old again. Michael taught himself to be a tattoo artist. After I divorced Ole, Michael gave me a tattoo: a symbol of love and pain. Michael taught himself a lot of skills: martial arts, Chinese healing methods, and other disciplines and aspects of Asian culture. And he played pool like no one else. In 2017, Michael died of an aggressive form of cancer. Like me, he hated doctors and waited too long to see one. I was with him on his deathbed. I held his hand until the very end, just as he always held mine. I was devastated by his death—I couldn't stop crying. Even as I write this now, I'm crying.

Michael had a lot of children: eight, in fact, with four different women. Most of his children are over eighteen now, although not all of them are faring well. It's hard to watch history repeat itself. I know Michael's resources—I remember quite well how he took care of his three siblings when he was only thirteen—but now I can't do much more than observe and be whatever family and support I can be.

And then there's Mom. Richard died when Mom was sixty-six. Mom was with him and took care of him until the end. The violence abated as the years passed, and ultimately they lived a rather peaceful life. The day Richard died, Mom called, unhappy. I grabbed Magnus and Tea and drove quickly to Lolland to comfort her. Stepping into the apartment, we encountered a thick cloud of smoke and the loud rattle of bottles. Inside the room sat five or six people, all of them in high spirits, including Mom and my brother Michael. Someone shoved a beer in my hand, and once we oriented ourselves, we saw Richard lying dead on a bed against one of the walls. That was a shock for both the children and me: the scene was completely grotesque. It got even more grotesque when one of the mangy drunks offered me his chair as he hopped up on the end of Richard's bed so we could sit down. Mom floated around, now and then walking over to caress Richard's cheek. She seemed unaffected.

Mom died last year of lung cancer at the age of seventy-three, four days before my fiftieth birthday. As with Monkey, I sat by her bed and held her hand until she died. For almost a year, I took her to cancer treatments, and we had some fine conversations along the way. She admitted she had seen Jan's abuse and apologized. It was a good year— and when she finally died in her sleep, I felt calm. I never forgave her, but in the course of that year, I began to understand how it could have gone so far.

Dad lives in southern France; he married another woman, Astrid, and they return home a couple of times a year. Sometimes we get together; sometimes we don't. At times in my adult life, I haven't wanted to see him. I'm still so angry that he left me to that hell in Lolland. It flares up regularly—but thank God not as often now.

Dad's had quite a career in the labor movement, and my half siblings have done really well with associate degrees and jobs. I've seen them at different times, although none of them came to René's funeral—which finally made me realize there's a difference between the "right" and "wrong" children. Yes, we were the wrong children who were always in trouble. But I could have used a strong, healthy family to support Tonny, Michael, and me after we said goodbye to René.

Mom and Dad were at the funeral, and I was furious from the moment I stepped into the church until I was back in the car. I felt like throwing up when Mom threw herself, crying, on top of the coffin. If only they'd shown him that kind of attention when he was living. He was barely in the ground before they started discussing who'd have to pay for the gravestone.

I often say I'm "reasonably disturbed" in many areas because of my upbringing. For example, I continue to struggle with having faith in others. I always have one foot out the door, an escape route—yet, Mikael and I have been together for twelve years now and married for five of them. Last summer we moved in together. We did so with great trepidation, but I love every minute we're together—and I feel secure, which is a giant step forward for me.

Another thing I continue to struggle with is low self-esteem. As chair of the National Council for Children, I was criticized quite harshly now and then for some of my decisions. It's only natural—yet those criticisms hit me hard. On several occasions, I'd burst into tears because of these critiques, fortunately only in places where people could handle it. Being open with the children's council secretariat about my upbringing was an immense help: they knew they were dealing with a somewhat idiosyncratic personality, one possessed of both strength and vulnerability. They knew they had to take that last part into consideration.

There's one thing I know I'm good at—and that's raising children. I have a large brood of strong, healthy, and unique children, all of whom have gotten at least one of my character traits. Several of my acquaintances have commented on it.

Asbjørn and Magnus got my sensitivity—that heightened awareness of other people. As boys, it made them cautious and quite empathetic; with age, however, it's transformed into a deep insight and a capacity for strong leadership. As mentioned earlier, Asbjørn is a father and an officer, and Magnus will start high school this year.

Ida has my sense of accomplishment: she's always coordinating and arranging things that her peers would never be able to handle. Whenever Ole or I aren't there, she assumes the parental role, which others assign to her naturally. She's tough but fair. She's studying to work with youth in an after-school center, and she's also managing a nightclub.

Freja has my impertinence, that lust for life and faith in herself. She's making a name for herself as a musician—and she and I have written a children's book together.

Tea? She's all kindness and order, seasoned with high ethical standards. She's also gotten a touch of my angst, but most of the time she uses it constructively to ensure that nothing goes wrong. If I want to be certain that something's going to get done, she's the one I entrust the job to. After she finishes high school, she plans to go into the service, most likely the navy.

Common among all of them is sweetness, gentleness, openness, and faith in others. I didn't discover the latter in myself until I was an adult, but they've had it from the start. It's exciting to see how they manage their very strange inheritance from me.

My children have asked me several times why they aren't named Zornig, like me. I tell them I didn't want to pass on the legacy of that name. I needed the name: I had to use that anger to liberate myself from my own personal inheritance. Born into light and love, my children don't need that anger. On the other hand, my nephews and nieces still need the name: they could stand a little more anger, a little more Zornig.

No need for them to know that some relatives say they mustn't use the name Zornig: that's what I was told on my Facebook wall when I spoke about my family's alcohol problems shortly after being named chair of the National Council for Children. I was informed that part of my father's family—Zornigs—didn't want to be identified with me. Unfortunately for them, it's a fact of life—just as it was a fact of life for me to grow up in a living hell.

I am and will always be a Zornig. And I'm angry.

HOW DO WE BREAK THE PATTERN?

In the rest of this book, I've avoided writing as the former chair of Denmark's National Council for Children. Here, though, I'd like to discuss what society can learn from my story and what adults who work with victimized and neglected children and teens can do to help break the typical pattern of the abused child's life—to change values and morals, not merely education and wage bracket.

Before I wrote this book, I had clear ideas about how to break the pattern. That hasn't really changed, but I realize there's a factor I haven't given that much weight to: the fire or energy residing in each person.

For me it was anger. That could have easily been my downfall, but along the way I met people who acknowledged and supported me; they helped me to divert my anger and energy in constructive ways. Anger motivated my constant insistence on getting a good education. Does that fire burn in all victimized children? Yes, basically, I think it does. Unfortunately, that fire is extinguished for many children, because they never meet the right people—or else it's channeled into destructive behavior because they meet the wrong people. For the vast majority, however, there is hope, right up to the end of their childhood.

In my view, five essential factors must be present to help break the pattern. The first is the *fire* that must exist within each child. It has to be capable of being ignited. It must be present in order for you to reach these children and grab their attention, their desire, and their faith in life and in the adults around them. I believe all children are born with energy—with a yearning to grow as a person. Victimized children have it too. Perhaps they hide it well, or even worse, it surfaces as negative energy, manifesting itself in destructive and hateful behavior. Despite serious neglect, these children preserve a small flicker of fire deep inside, and with patience, it can be found and nourished. Therefore, it's my conviction that most children who've been abused and betrayed for many years can still—with the right help—hope for a bright future.

As long as there's life, caregivers must act under the assumption that wounds can be healed, just as doctors are obligated to attempt to save lives, regardless of the prognosis. Unfortunately, it's been my experience that people tend to reject neglected children right from the start, so they can never have a normal life.

By the time I showed up at Hylleholt—a disturbed fourteen-year-old girl—Lolland had already rejected me. Thank God I got another chance; within four years, Hylleholt managed to achieve what normally takes an entire childhood. That happened because they believed the anger and destructive behavior from my time in Lolland could be turned into something positive.

The second factor that must exist to break the pattern is *love*—a *personal relationship* between at least one strong, stable adult and the vulnerable child. I don't believe that love is reserved solely for adults and children with the same blood. Love can be expressed in many forms—and it can be nurtured.

It's imperative that children feel that someone cares about them. Misses them. Is happy for them. Especially neglected children. Love is a basic human need that professional caregivers often lack any training in. Fortunately, it comes naturally to many—but it's still a long road to getting love onto the schedule at teachers colleges and at job interviews when hiring personnel for schools, institutions, and foster care.

Along the way, I experienced many forms of love, from Karen, Rigmor, the butcher, Holst, and all the others who showed me that I mattered. I felt it when someone lit up when I entered a room. Many of us are good at showing our children this kind of love, at letting them know that they matter.

The third factor is *faith* in each child. People are equipped with a natural urge to develop, which means we grow best in an appropriate—and safe—environment. That's an important starting point when working with victimized children. We must never assume that it's only natural for children to behave destructively. In my view, it's unnatural and probably a consequence of harmful betrayal and growing up in a hostile environment. Just like other people, these children want to succeed and be happy—there's always something to build upon when working with vulnerable children. To draw that "something" out, however, you must show faith in the child, even when she's behaving strangely.

Look at my need for approval from boys and men—and my desire to return to Nakskov and the environment I came from. My files reveal that Hylleholt decided to let me go back to Nakskov until I discovered for myself that I no longer needed to. My excesses might just as well have resulted in the school forbidding me from going back there, but that never happened. They had faith in me—faith that I could handle it and that I'd come to them when I needed help severing ties with my former environment. Which I did, eventually.

What's wonderful about having faith in these children is that they begin to exhibit faith in their surroundings. It's a slow process in which boundaries and failures must be tested. The neglected child often wonders: Will my social worker like me even when I fail? Social workers who go the distance can expect a miracle of faith.

The fourth necessary factor is a constant and insistent *focus on education*. Victimized children have roughly five to eighteen years to get a foothold. After that, it's basically the young person's own responsibility to manage. On their path to adulthood, teens who've had a normal upbringing have a network of adults who support and advise them, both practically and mentally. Neglected children, on the other hand, often experience only a fragile network of adults to help with their education and employment.

Therefore, education must become a major focus until these children turn eighteen—no matter how late each child is discovered and helped. In my own case, I was lucky, because I loved doing schoolwork. Still, regardless of their interest or joy in school, all neglected youth must receive an education—even if they have to have their hand held every day. Without education, any personal relation with or faith in a young person is irrelevant: they still turn eighteen lacking the skills to become self-reliant adults—and they have a greater risk of social problems as a consequence of poverty and the absence of any professional identity.

The fifth and final factor necessary to break the pattern is that we must *listen to each child*. According to the UN Convention on the Rights of the Child, children must be heard, which is reason enough to do so. In addition, it's my firm conviction that better solutions are found when children—like adults—are heard. The fact that a child accepts any effort means you're halfway to your goal. We can predict the outcome of a child's first meeting with a mentor or institution of care by whether or not the child grasps the proposed solution. So the effort must be made here. Also, I truly believe that children and teens often know what's good for them—especially when they find themselves in a trusting atmosphere. Along with our lack of faith in children's natural drive to develop, people often overlook the fact that children are experts on their own lives.

Was I heard? Mostly not, until I turned fourteen. Files from my time in the orphanage in Nakskov reveal that for two years I repeatedly asked to be placed in a foster family. My requests were denied, initially with the explanation that my mother was afraid of losing her connection to me. They eventually rejected my request because they said I had too many issues for a foster family—despite the fact that the psychologist who'd created my psychological profile when I arrived at the orphanage recommended placement with a foster family. No one was listening to me, and I reacted as many teens do—by resisting. They interpreted my resistance as guilt for my own problems. The reason given for not placing me with a family was that I needed to learn how to behave properly—not that my parents had exposed me to neglect.

When I arrived at Hylleholt, a whole world of compassion and respect for my attitudes and limitations opened up for me. Not that everything that ensued was totally unproblematic. Still, at Hylleholt I always felt that they were trying to understand my behavior—that they had the best possible motives and were trying to meet me halfway whenever they could.

There's no guarantee, but I believe that caregivers can best help the neglected child or teen when they remember the following:

Find the fire.
Give love.
Show faith.
Support education.
Listen to the child.

AFTERWORD

Hans Christian Andersen's fairy tale about the ugly duckling begins in a duck yard and ends on a lake, where the beautiful swan sees its reflection in the water. The moral: it doesn't matter if you're born in a duck yard, as long as you are hatched from a swan's egg!

Another story dealing with this theme is Henrik Pontoppidan's "Eagle's Flight." In this tale, an eagle starts its life in a chicken coop but is shot by a stable hand as it lifts its wings to fly away. The moral: it's no use being an eagle when you're born in a chicken coop.

Which story do *you* believe? That depends on your view of human nature—and of society.

As I read Lisbeth Zornig Andersen's story, I realize that neither of the aforementioned tales offers the ultimate truth, even though I'm drawn to the first about the beautiful swan. Fortunately for her readers, Lisbeth's story begins where Hans Christian Andersen's ends. As readers, when we already know there's a happy ending, it becomes easier to stare into the duck yard where the story begins. And in this case, that beginning is grim.

Three-year-old Lisbeth lets us peer into a world few of us will recognize—even though it exists just around every corner and not simply on the Danish island of Lolland. We proceed with the four-year-old Lisbeth as our guide, then the five-year-old, and so on. We continue peering into this world until the eighteen-year-old Lisbeth steps formally into the ranks of adulthood and leaves what has never really been a childhood.

It goes from bad to worse. It starts with betrayal—and these betrayals only multiply. Just when we see a glimmer of hope that someone will do something to rescue the little girl from the chaos of destitution—alcoholism, violence, abuse, and gross neglect—we are soon disappointed, and the little girl is betrayed yet again.

Most stories have both heroes and villains, but there are fewer heroes in Lisbeth's story. The indignation the book awakens in readers compels us to search for villains—and we find many who fit the bill. Yet it's difficult to lay blame in one place. What has happened and not happened in Lisbeth's childhood cannot be reversed.

Some people in Lolland probably developed nervous tics when this book was first published. In my mind, that's not really important. What's important is that we act on the indignation the book awakens within us—that we understand that we *can* make a difference in a child's life. Even though Lisbeth's story isn't teeming with heroes who step in and end the neglect and abuse, we still meet a number of people who react compassionately to what any eye could see: an undernourished child with warts and conjunctivitis, with strange wounds on her arms, wearing sandals in the winter. All these people have made a difference, large or small, which Lisbeth takes note of: they've given her some hope that, yes, life just might be worthwhile.

As fellow human beings, we must also take on that responsibility. Do *something* when we meet a neglected child, at the very least indicate that we have *seen* and *understood* what's happening.

When they hear Lisbeth's story through her lectures, professionals dealing with victimized children and families become deeply engaged in trying to figure out how Lisbeth was able to break the pattern of the neglected child. How was she able to trade the barstool for the executive chair? Their interest is anything but surprising: they hope to learn something about methods in social work by analyzing such a unique case.

Of course, it would be a lot easier if we were talking about a single event or specific person responsible for the ultimate turning point in Lisbeth's life. Instead, hers has been a long and painful developmental process, during which some people have been in the right place at the right time for her.

I'm not an impartial reader: I'm a person in the book, and I've known Lisbeth's story for many years, albeit in smaller pieces. So, I, too, have shared this professional curiosity—but no more. I've stopped looking for explanations. I can only concur with Urie Bronfenbrenner when he says:

"A child needs the enduring, irrational involvement of one or more adults in care of and in joint activity with that child. In short, *somebody has to be crazy about that kid.*"

Karen Gjesing
Social worker and coach

ARTICLE 12

1. States Parties shall assure to the child who is capable of forming his or her own views the right to express those views freely in all matters affecting the child, the views of the child being given due weight in accordance with the age and maturity of the child.

2. For this purpose, the child shall in particular be provided the opportunity to be heard in any judicial and administrative proceedings affecting the child, either directly, or through a representative or an appropriate body, in a manner consistent with the procedural rules of national law.

United Nations Convention on the Rights of the Child

ACKNOWLEDGMENTS

I'd like to thank a number of people who helped make this book possible. Thank you to my children and to Ole, their father and my best friend, for living with a very distracted and absent mother and friend who made great demands on their time and patience.

Thank you to my husband, Mikael, for patiently supporting me and guiding me through writing my first book—and for crying with me as I wrote about the worst experiences.

Thanks to the many heroes in my childhood—you'll meet them in the book.

Thanks to the many people I've drawn on for the energy and courage to write about the unmentionable. I know they'll still like me, even after reading this book, and that means the world to me.

And thank you to Amazon Crossing for publishing my story in English, so that more people can read it, and to Mark Mussari for translating it with empathy and loyalty.

ABOUT THE AUTHOR

Lisbeth Zornig Andersen is a former children's ombudsman in Denmark and the author of the bestselling memoir *Anger Is My Middle Name*, her first work to be translated into English. Already well known in Denmark for her advocacy and for *My Childhood in Hell*, a documentary detailing her early years, Lisbeth received global recognition in 2015 when she was charged and later sentenced for picking up a family of Syrian refugees in her car. This simple act of charity earned coverage in such publications as the *Washington Post*, *Le Monde*, the *Guardian*, and the *Huffington Post* and on air at the BBC and Al Jazeera, igniting an international debate about the ethics and legality of humanitarian aid. Lisbeth has also founded her own advisory consultancy and charitable foundation, where she continues her socially centered work.

ABOUT THE TRANSLATOR

Mark Mussari has his PhD in Scandinavian languages and literature from the University of Washington in Seattle. He has translated Danish novels, short stories, and nonfiction for publication, including Dan Turèll's seminal crime novel, *Murder in the Dark*. A scholar of Danish literature, art, and design, Mussari is the author of numerous academic journal articles and the book *Danish Modern: Between Art and Design*. Mussari is also the author of numerous educational books, including books on Haruki Murakami, Amy Tan, Shakespeare's *Othello* and sonnets, and popular culture. His recent translations for Amazon Crossing include Erik Valeur's *The Man in the Lighthouse* and Carsten Jensen's *The First Stone*.